HEALING
CONNECTIONS

RECONCILING A BROKEN WORLD
TO A HOLY AND LOVING GOD

Dr. Lisa Kohut, Ed.D, LCPC,CADC

Healing Connections: Reconciling a Broken World to a Holy and Loving God

www.positiveoutcomesconsulting.com

ISBN-9781730702662

edited by Water2WinePress Publishing House,
a Subsidiary of Ink Well Spoken

CONTENTS

"He planned for the maturity of the times and the climax of the ages to unify all things and head them up and consummate them in Christ, both things in heaven and things on the earth."

– Ephesians 1:10 (Amplified Version)

Blessing/Warning: As you read the pages of this book, you will notice an impartation of Love, Unity, Peace and Connection. You will notice your eyes being opened to things that they were once closed to and you will become aware of ways or ideas to apply some of these principles in your spheres of influence. When that occurs, don't ignore it or deny it, it's the purpose of this book and my prayer for every person who takes the time to read this book.

ACKNOWLEDGEMENTS

would like to express my sincere gratitude to several individuals who have encouraged, supported, inspired, believed in, prayed for me and given me any kind of enlightenment that has helped me along this path. First, I would like to thank the Holy Spirit, for partnering with me in writing this book and for allowing me to be a vessel to express the heart of God. I would also like to thank my mom, who has gone to Glory, but who has always been my biggest and loudest cheerleader in every corner of life. Thank you for always believing in me, having so much confidence in my ability to do whatever I commit my mind to and for expressing that confidence in such a loving way. You have been an incredible source of inspiration, motivation, confidence and faith in my life. It has been the influence of my mom's love that has inspired me to write this book. I would also like to thank my Dad for his patient love and for always encouraging me and believing in me. I would also like to thank you for continuing to push me toward my ultimate goal and for your many, many words of wisdom that have been very applicable throughout life. I would like to thank all of my family and siblings for every ounce of support that you've given me throughout the years and I would like to thank every person whose story contributed to this book in any way.

Finally, I would like to thank Reggie Kee, my editor. Thank you for allowing the Holy Spirit to guide you in our partnership to make this book the most excellent it can be.

PHYSICAL CONNECTIONS

THE INVITATION

t was the summer of 2014 and the Holy Spirit was inviting me to partner with Him in private practice; effectively ending my 11-year employment at a therapeutic school in Highland Park, IL as a school psychologist. Not at all comfortable with God's timing, I built up a case of rebuttals revolving around how inconvenient such a leap of faith would be for me:

- I didn't have a website

- I didn't have a business plan

- I had no office space

- I didn't have much capital to start a business

(or clientele for that matter)

- I would go from two paychecks per month to… what?

- Speaking of "what's"… what if I'm not effective?

- I refuse to be the type of therapist who holds clients for years without seeing any fruit or significant results

- Did I mention how untimely and inconvenient this move would be?

God's response to my laundry list of countering was simple but profound: "Healing is in the Connection." I wasn't clear on what He meant by that so I asked for some clarification and He responded by saying: "The symptoms of dis-ease that we've seen in mankind (including anxiety, depression, etc.) were really related to some form of disconnection from Me, disconnection from self, or disconnection from community." That sounded profound but what did that have to do with the immediate concern of leaving my job, Jesus?

THE FACTS

According to census data the National Institute of Mental Health (NIMH) taken in 2016, approximately 18.1 percent (40 million) of adults between the ages of 18-54 have sought some form of help due to struggling with anxiety disorders. Said statistic increases 30% if we include people who struggle but don't seek help for various reasons. According to separate studies from both Dr. Daniel Amen (2015) and the United Kingdom's Minister for Loneliness, 9 million British people report feeling lonely to some degree. Some have called loneliness and social isolation an epidemic which affects people's emotional and physical health. In other words, having people in your life who care about and interact with you regularly may reduce the likelihood of developing colds, cognitive decline or depression. Additionally, a longitudinal study at Harvard University followed hundreds of people for 75 years and found that the best predictor of physical health, quality of life and longevity was the quality of people's relationships. Both the statistics and the experiment seem to conclude that meaningful connection is the single most effective and powerful mechanism that we can build into our lives to minimize or eliminate the effects of illness; thus improving our quality of life.

One thing that neither the stats nor the study reveal however, which is the premise of this book, is that sustaining disconnection from God, others and self is the largest contributing factor to the symptoms chronicled by such studies. This detachment, which has become so pervasive in society, far too often goes unnoticed until physical, emotional, spiritual and mental symptoms surface and become almost unbearable, or consequently lead to death. These symptoms, albeit inconvenient and uncomfortable, have a way of unwittingly steering us back to reconnect to the true Source of our relational strength, which is our Heavenly Father by way of Jesus Christ and the Holy Spirit.

THE CONNECTION MESSAGE

Have you ever noticed how God emphasized the importance of connection and relationships from the very beginning? God the Father wasn't even alone! Even after He stated in Genesis 1:26 "Let US make man in OUR image, after OUR likeness" (emphasis added), He created mankind (male and female) in the very next verse! He created us as relational beings from the beginning and intended for us to live in harmony with Him and one another as we maintained heaven and earth in peaceful coexistence. I believe this is why when the Word of God came on the scene as Jesus and was asked which commandment is the most important, He responded with wisdom that we ought to "Love the Lord your God with all your heart and with all your soul and with all your strength and with all your mind; and love your neighbor as yourself" (see Matthew 22:37 and Luke 10:27).

The One Who created the heavens and the earth provided us a big clue that the key to peace and wholeness is staying connected to Him, ourselves, and others in a meaningful and peaceful way. This, however, can be a challenging task when we live in a culture that seems so disconnected.

God has created us to not only desire but to thrive the most while relating to and maintaining peace with one another. Biologically, our brains have been wired with receptors that, when functioning correctly, support relational connections with God and people as well as sabotage those very same relationships when they're not functioning as God intended them (Lehman, 2016). Plainly stated, when these relationship receptors are on, we feel ready to connect with God and others. Contrarily, when they're partially or completed shut down, we don't feel connected to others and may not even have the desire to connect; as we may not even be able to see the need for connections – divine or otherwise (Lehman, 2016). Beyond these receptors in our neural network, we also have a limbic system that responds accordingly when we improve our emotional bonds with others; impacting our mood for the better or for the worse based on how connected we are with others.

THE BIG PICTURE

Nowhere else in the scriptures does God identify the importance of the separate body parts functioning together as a community more than in 1 Corinthians 12:13-27. Further still, verse 26 specifically used the word "suffer" (seen as the word "hurt" in the passage) to describe the adverse impact which could occur when individuals operate separate from one another:

> **"The way God designed our bodies is a model for understanding our lives together in relationships, as a family and as a church: every part dependent on every other part, the parts we mention and the parts we don't, the parts we see and the parts we don't. If one part hurts, every other part is involved**

in the hurt, and in the healing. If one part flourishes, every other part enters into the exuberance."

– 1 Corinthians 12:25-26

(The Message Version)

This emphasis is magnified once the realization sets in that this anatomical metaphor was really discussing the way in which we interact with one another within the church community. But why was such importance given to relationship and connection? There must be a very important reason. If we look to science, we'll find that research has shown that the very particles we're made of, though they appear to be separate, interact as if connected. To drive home the point further, think of the last time you stubbed your pinky toe. Something as seemingly insignificant as the pinky toe can dramatically impact the body as a whole if it is injured; as it provides balance to our bodies when we walk. Yet, when it comes to viewing the church as one body interconnected in a similar way, the thought of us all being affected by each other's hurts (from the greatest to the least of us) is more challenging to embrace.

After all, from mere appearances, it looks like and feels

as if we're all separate – even though the Word tells us that through God's Holy Spirit, we are many members connected as one body in Christ Jesus. This big picture concept becomes even more challenging, ironically, the more we are plugged into the dysfunctional world system that both surrounds and desensitizes us to the importance of spiritual connection to our heavenly Father.

THE EVIDENCE OF CONNECTION IN NATURE

According to scientists, fungi, which was once thought to be a tree infection, has been found to have integral significance to a tree's root system. Fungus enhances a tree's connection to the earth through fungal tubes which break up the soil while weaving into tree roots at the cellular level. Interconnectivity in the plant kingdom plays out on a grand scale ecologically, as well. Within a given ecosystem, individual plants are joined together by an underground network - known as the "wood-wide web." This network allows fungi and plants to exchange resources and even send warnings to one another. This level of connection has caused scientists to see the forest as a superorganism as opposed to simply a collection of individual plants. This is yet more evidence pointing to the fact that God's relational design is not only for humans but for the world, as well. However, we can't fully benefit from the beauty of the big picture while still existing as disjointed puzzle pieces that refuse to correct the issue of disconnection.

WHAT DO I MEAN BY DISCONNECTION?

My earliest memory of disconnection occurred on a field trip with my first grade class. I felt so alone, so unloved and so rejected. Though no one was being mean to me, I felt different and ashamed of being the only black kid on the bus. Based on my feelings of "being different," I decided that I didn't "fit in" and wouldn't be accepted, so I stayed quiet and distant. I made the decision in my heart that being different was bad in some way; consequently, it brought shame which then caused me to hide just as Adam and Eve hid from God upon disobeying Him – only, I hadn't done anything wrong.

As uncomfortable and lonely as being disconnected can be, I believe that it's a decision we all make at some point in order to protect ourselves. We all have what seems like legitimate reasons for isolating ourselves. Many reasons keep us disconnected from others, which can eventually lead to physical, mental, emotional, spiritual and financial breakdowns. According to Daniels and Price (2018), we have each developed a defensive mechanism to protect a specific aspect of our psyches that felt vulnerable while our personality was being developed. The study of this protective process brought about the identification of nine ("ennea" in Greek) interconnected personality types within an individual which has become known as the Enneagram of Personality. Those nine personalities are the: reformer, helper, achiever, individualist, investigator, loyalist, enthusiast and challenger.

The bad news is that with so many personality types within us and a community comprised of so many individuals, it seems inevitable that too many moving parts within a system will eventually fail. The good news is that a breakdown is often necessary before a breakthrough can occur! In other words, it's often in our brokenness that we're willing to empty ourselves of ourselves (whether it be as individuals or as a society) – putting us in the perfect position to be filled up with the wisdom of God.

THE ORIGIN OF DISCONNECTION

After choosing to eat from the tree of the knowledge of good and evil, Adam and Eve presented with symptoms of fear and shame in Genesis 3:6-7; which led them to try to hide from God's presence in the Garden of Eden. After eating from this tree, their consciousness shifted from oneness with God's consciousness to the isolation of self-consciousness. Simply put, the fear crept in because they no longer felt connected to God. Upon shifting from being naked and transparent before the Lord to feeling disconnected, shame joined the fear; as they desired to hide from the presence of God (though the physical state of their nakedness had not changed prior to them eating the fruit). When God confronted their disunion, Adam and Eve confessed their fear and hiding (alluding to their shame) and attempted to cover it all up with not only fig leaves but with a faulty reasoning that pointed towards the sudden awareness of their nakedness. God, being the omniscient Father that He is, knew exactly what to ask them; resulting in what can easily be identified as the first psychological assessment in history! He got right to the root of the problem by simply asking: "Who told you that you were naked?" (See Genesis 3:11).

God did not focus on the symptoms of fear and shame because that wasn't the real issue. The issue was the introduction and new knowledge of a perceived evil resulting from the consumption of a fruit that God had told them not to eat. Thus fear and shame were symptoms of something even larger. The sin of disobedience (listening to a talking serpent versus God) was at the core of Adam and Eve's disconnection. Eating from this tree opened their self-conscious eyes; allowing the world's first dysfunctional married couple to judge their condition without the wisdom of their sovereign Father which introduced them (and us) to a level of folly that God never intended. Obeying this sin-inducing serpent (that would later be identified as the devil in Revelation 12:9) opened the door to biased judgment and faulty condemnation of self and others; which has effectively driven mankind to hide from God and one another ever since. Such separation even foreshadows an inability to forgive which will be further expounded on in Chapter 6.

Returning to the root cause of Adam and Eve's downfall, when the serpent invited Eve to eat from the tree of knowledge of good and evil, it introduced a life devoid of peace and rife with disconnection: riddled by cursed covenants with God and broken relationships with people. The moment Eve disconnected from God to obey evil, Adam and Eve's life shifted from eternal to temporal; from perfection and righteousness to imperfection and unrighteousness – The serpent invited Adam and Eve into the realm of separation. The real question that you may be asking yourself as you read this is: But what does this have to do with anxiety, depression and disease in individuals, families, communities and the church?

Disconnection and disease begin the same way now, as it did in the Garden of Eden when the world's first power couple chose to disobey and disconnect from God's presence. The first disconnection that needs to be restored today is the same one that needed to be restored in the garden state: the disconnection of our true identity from God. The second and third disconnection are from ourselves and from others. When we're disconnected from God, our earthly relationships become increasingly challenging; hence, the next step after restoring our fellowship with God is to restore our fellowship with ourselves and others. The first restoration should make the final two very simple; for true peace (within ourselves and with others) is found through reconnecting with God.

Throughout the rest of this book, I'll discuss the principles of peace and connection that the Holy Spirit has revealed to me over the years. These principles have been very effective in sustaining peace in my life and relationships and helping others to obtain and sustain peace in their lives and relationships, as well. The foundation and glue of connection is having a relationship with God through Jesus Christ which is then sealed by the Holy Spirit. And so, having walked through the introductory chapter of this book, you and I both now have the answer as to why God had prompted me to leave my job. In fact, He wasn't asking me to leave as much as He had prepared me to expand the scope and reach of my purpose in life which far exceeds the boundaries of my former employment.

CHAPTER

THE ILLUSION OF SEPARATION

Science lends empirical evidence allowing us to assert that separation isn't real – rather, it is imagined. Meaning the mind deceives us into perceiving separation based on previous experiences, lies, or messages and creates the feeling of being alone. A problem arises with this coping mechanism in that it creates a false reality that lulls us into forgetting that we are still, in fact, connected. The solution to this problem is found in remembering that we were originally made to be one with our Creator; with all of humanity tracing its origin back to one man which means… we're all connected. Yes – we are definitely NOT EVER alone!

In the Joe Vitale's book *Zero Limits: The Secret Hawaiian System for Wealth, Peace, and More* (2007), there's a true story about a therapist in Hawaii who healed clients without seeing them. Though he worked at the Hawaii State Hospital for 4 years with the criminally insane, he didn't physically meet with most or any of the inmates. Instead, he reviewed their files and took full responsibility for any presented condition that had been documented. In doing so, he was able to get positive results.

Sound interesting? I thought it might! Here's how he did it. After he noted the condition of a given patient, Dr. Hew Len would take responsibility by meditating on the following: "I love you. I'm sorry. Please forgive me. Thank you." Dr. Hew Len subscribed to the practice of Ho'oponopono which taught that when someone showed up with a problem, the practitioner had the power to address the problem by first accepting that the practitioner must have a memory in common with the patient's affliction; else the practitioner would not be able to see the illness of the patient. Using this methodology, Dr. Hew Len focused on healing others by first healing himself which supports the scientific evidence suggesting that we're all connected. As a direct result of his intervention at the hospital, according to Dr. Joe Vitale, of *Zero Limits,* the entire ward closed down because he had allegedly managed to help the inmates to improve or eradicate symptoms of mental illness. I believe Dr. Hew Len showcased the concept of oneness to its fullest. Instead of seeing someone else's issue only as THEIR problem, his solution approached it as OUR problem; thus, deconstructing the illusion of separation.

Subsequently, if I see us as connected and your problem as my problem, then I have access to the power to heal myself and I can effectually heal both of us at the same time. Though Dr. Hew Len does not proclaim to be a Christian, he has managed to tap into something powerful that the church may be missing. Though Jesus exemplified this approach by taking OUR sins as HIS own: peace and freedom (from disconnected, diseased lifestyles) begins with you. Is this not what Romans 2:1 reflected?

> **"You may think you can condemn such people, but you are just as bad, and you have no excuse! When you say they are wicked and should be punished, you are condemning yourself, for you judge others and do these very same things."**

In order for one person to judge another in this manner, the person judging must have entered into a flawed knowledge of good and evil, which is the tree or way of life that we were instructed to avoid. Such a realm exists for mankind because the enemy introduced it to mankind through Eve thousands upon thousands of years ago and has assigned accusers to remind the brethren of the shame of this original sin (see Revelation 12:10). False judgment of our fellow brothers and sisters (to whom we are connected) aligns us with the greatest weapon of our spiritual accusers and drives a wedge of separation between us and our Kingdom family. Jesus warned against this weapon of division when He stated that "a house divided against itself cannot stand" (see Matthew 12:25). In other words, the house of God is the Kingdom of God or the church and family of God. As long as the people who make up the church are divided as evidenced by slandering, accusing or judging one another, our house or the Kingdom is divided and it will have no influence on the world because the world will see the church in the same condition or worse than the world. Earlier in the book of Matthew, we see the perils of biased judgment, as well:

> **"Do not judge others, and you will not be judged, for you will be treated as you treat others. The standard you use in judging is the standard by which you will be judged.**

And why worry about a speck in your friend's eye when you have a log in your own?"

– Matthew 7:1-3

Returning to Dr. Hew Len's judgment-free method for a moment, According to Dr. Vitale (2007), patients within the hospital ward began presenting amazing proof of improvement of their symptoms of disassociated diseases. Those who were once shackled now walked freely. Medication prescriptions reduced. Inmates who were once hopeless about being released were being freed. Even the staff morale began to improve! The answer appears evident but the question becomes this: What if this is how unity and oneness is supposed to look in our communities and churches? Dr. Hew Len's approach eliminated judging individuals (of whom communities and churches are comprised) which is often a barrier to connection because it reinforces unforgiveness and creates obstacles to reconciliation. The theory he executed revolved around the notion that humanity has become addicted to the idea that someone else's problems are outside of our sphere of influence. Instead of feeding into this, Dr. Hew Len chose to believe that problems which exist in others exist in us; which means that we have an opportunity to address individual afflictions as a network just as the plants and trees within a forest share and process information to maintain the overall health of the ecosystem. I think Maya Angelou summed it up very well when she said the following words: "I am human, nothing human can be alien to me".

Question: Do you see another person's problems as outside of your sphere of influence or do you recognize a sense of responsibility to address them as a part of our shared inheritance of sin? If your answer leaned on the former, can you see this as an issue of disconnection/separation? I believe that our beliefs about our sins and others will dictate how we approach the issue in ourselves and others. Ecology, psychology and theology aside, science validates these findings, as well. I believe that our beliefs about our sins and others will dictate how we approach the issue with ourselves and others.

Dr. Hew Len's results unknowingly reinforced the scientific theory of the Observer Effect. In quantum physics, the Observer Effect says that subatomic matter doesn't exist until it is seen. Experiments have proven that quantum particles exist as waves of energy – showing up as particles of matter only at the point of observation. Hence, our acknowledgement of substance (immaterial or otherwise), contributes to its manifestation in the natural realm which is a precursor to our ability to affect it. I'm not suggesting that we go around pretending that the darkness of this world doesn't exist nor am I suggesting that we ignore it; rather, if we stopped blaming/judging others and accepted responsibility for how we've contributed or related to it (thus acknowledging the duality of our role within it as well as its role within us), perhaps we would be more adept at transforming darkness into light.

John 8:12-"I am the Light of the world. He who follows Me will not be walking in the dark, but will have the Light which is life" (Amplified version) and John 9:5 "As long as I am in the world, I am the world's Light" (Amplified version) recorded Jesus declaring Himself to be the light of the world. What if the way to reconcile everyone to Christ (therefore, transforming the darkness of the world into light) was through acknowledging others without distinguishing them as being separate from ourselves? What if remembering that we are all connected allowed us to both receive AND extend forgiveness – choosing to forget the ways in which someone else contributed to our need to forgive them? Doing so eliminates the way we tend to weigh our sins relative to someone else's. For some reason, we've managed to create a false sense of comfort in separation. This has caused us to believe that somehow we're superior to someone else based on the varying degrees of our sins which are based in shared yet shallow variables such as behavior, financial status, educational level, race, religion, etc. We would do well to remember what Romans 12:3 says:

> **"For by the grace (unmerited favor of God) given to me I warn everyone among you not to estimate and think of himself more highly than he ought (not to have an exaggerated opinion of his own importance), but to rate his ability with sober judgment, each according to the degree of faith apportioned by God to him." (Amplified Version)**

Are we living disconnected and diseased lifestyles because of our attachment to the illusion that we're all separate? Are we pretending to believe God when He says we're all one or, quite simply, have we grossly misinterpreted this truth found in Ephesians 2:14?

> **"For He is our peace. He has made us both (Jew and Gentile) one body, and has broken down (destroyed, abolished) the hostile dividing wall between us." (Amplified version)**

Have we been unwittingly subscribing to this theory of disconnection (the illusion of separation), all the while? Are we connected as one or separate but unequal? Is, in fact, separation just an illusion? Does it matter? And the final quandary in this line of questioning: Does the feeling or thought of being separate irredeemably downgrade us to a permanent state of disconnection?

There are some who revel in being loners from a Matrix-like world – where being unplugged is actually beneficial. However, to those individuals, I would argue that remaining isolated for extended periods of time invites such uncomfortable emotions as fear, hatred, anxiety, rejection and depression that can become difficult to ward off. Why? Because to be totally isolated is to be removed from love.

Perfect love casts out fear (see 1 John 4:18). Further still Romans 8:38-39 states:

> **"I am persuaded beyond doubt that neither life nor death, nor angels, nor principalities, nor powers, nor things present, nor things to come, nor height, nor depth, nor any other creatures, shall be able to separate me from**

the love of God, which is in Christ Jesus our Lord."

Recalling that 1 John 4:18 is preceded by the statement that God IS love in verse 8, it becomes evident that those who are in Christ cannot be separated from God's love. As such, when we experience sustained periods of the negative emotions listed at the end of the previous paragraph, we become more vulnerable to feeling disconnected from God and others in certain areas of our lives: specifically, areas that we haven't yielded to the Holy Spirit.

I believe there's an even deeper revelation regarding the mystery of our oneness with Him and with one another. Observe the following scriptures in concert:

> **"Make every effort to keep the unity of the Spirit through the bond of peace. There is one body and one Spirit, just as you were called to one hope when you were called; one Lord, one faith, one baptism;"**
>
> **– Ephesians 4:3-5**

> **"He is before all things, and in him all things hold together... and through him to reconcile**

to himself all things, whether things on earth or things in heaven, by making peace through his blood, shed on the cross. "

– Colossians 1:17, 20

Jesus made peace with everything in heaven and on earth which are then kept unified by the Holy Spirit. For those who have been reconciled to God through Christ, it is through our rebirth that we are now not only connected with God but with one another, as well. There is something powerful about this interconnectivity that the Bible has been communicating from the beginning which has somehow been lost in translation. For those who are proponents of separating science from the Bible, you may be disappointed to find that one supports the other in this regard.

We need look no further than the mysterious quantum realm (yet again!) to observe Biblical principles at work. According to the Entanglement Theory, making one change to a particle immediately affects the other particles no matter how far they are apart from each other. Rather, every move or decision we make influences even those whom we appear to be separated from. Einstein himself theorized relationships between gravity, space and time! But how can that be?

If it appears as though we're all physically separate, how can we really be connected as one? Perhaps the subatomic levels discussed in quantum physics is akin to the unseen spiritual realm discussed in the Bible. In layman's terms, if every substance known to man (consisting of atoms, molecules, DNA, etc.) was spoken into existence by the Word of God from an unseen realm, then doesn't it make sense that everything we see (people, objects, plants, animals, etc.) is related and connected from life's smallest building blocks up to the most complex life forms and systems known to man? Perhaps we are always interacting with and influencing everyone whether we know it or not because everything consists of the Word of God (see Colossians 1:17).

Imagine if we took this literally to the point that we actually ignite a global process of healing founded in our reconnection to God and one another? Is this what Jesus meant when He directed the disciples to pray "on earth as it is in heaven"? Let's be clear. We can become powerful beings that impact families, communities, churches and nations when we realize that other families, communities, churches and nations can't have a problem without it also being our problem, as well. Likewise, if there are those who have access to much needed answers through Christ, so too do others outside of our communities. That sounds like victory to me! Imagine the celebrations that would take place every time there was a healing or the unity that would occur when we truly understood that we're all in this together!

Allow me to redefine connection as a substance (going all the way down to the subatomic level) that is created between two or more people when they feel acknowledged (seen, known, heard and valued) in their pain. Beyond acknowledgment though, when we offer ourselves to one another as a means to help resolve the pain without judgment, this only deepens the connection:

> **"So in Christ we, though many, form one body, and each member belongs to all the others."**
>
> **– Romans 12:5**

the blessing of truly giving as we've received and listening as we've been heard knows no bounds. To be clear, this only works to the extent that we are willing to acknowledge the darkness in ourselves which the light of Christ remediates. In other words, a big part of the key to developing meaningful connections is the willingness to be vulnerable enough to recognize that darkness dwells in all of us yet can be overcome not by our might but by Jesus: the Light of the world and through the Grace of the Holy Spirit.

It behooves us all to be aware of this solution because this confirms that our prayers, intentions and thoughts can affect others as guided by Christ. I cannot emphasize enough that those of us who are stewards of God's Holy Spirit have the solution that the world around us desires to have. Let's make ourselves available to the Holy Spirit in a way that helps us to embrace and live a lifestyle of oneness that seeks out the brokenness of the world as broken vessels ourselves. Envision how your life and the lives of those around you would be different if we all began to see and respond to world issues from this perspective.

Let's change the world one decision at a time, one connection at a time. Let's choose to see from the truth that connects us.

CHAPTER

THE TRUE CAUSE
OF SEPARATION

THE TRUE CAUSE OF SEPARATION: DESPISING THE "LEAST OF THESE"

Beyond the illusion of separation, let's reaffirm the root of separation. The disobedience of sin and being consumed with self. However, that mainly deals with the separation between us and God. I'd like to approach a different angle regarding how we end up isolating ourselves from each other. It gets back to how we begin to differentiate one another into a caste system of sins which delineates the greatest from the least among us in the estimation of men. Though God sees all sin as equal defiance against His righteousness, we've warped our sense of sin (think back to the knowledge of good and evil) by associating the least sin(s) to the greatest among us and the greatest sin(s) to the least among us. We even see this in our criminal justice system with the distinction between crime and "white-collar" crime, which is allegedly better than other crimes.

When you think of the "least of these" in our culture, who do you think of? Take a moment to see who comes to mind in the following people groups:

- Your family   - Your country

- Your neighborhood   - Your child's school

- Your community   - The nations

Who came to mind? Perhaps it was that one drunk uncle that everyone has in their family. Maybe it was a neighbor who doesn't follow the rules of the association as meticulously as you do which is driving down your property value. Surely, the homeless or the criminally-minded in your community are holding back the prestige of your city; with a close runner-up being the mentally-imbalanced patients and single mothers clogging up our healthcare and welfare systems, respectively.

We can all agree that illegal immigrants are taking advantage of this country (of immigrants), right? Nobody likes a bully or takes the time to understand the student who always distracts the class and takes up the most time from your child's teacher. Lastly, who would be wrong in denoting the tyrants and terrorists amongst the nations as the lowest of the world? Please forgive the sarcasm as I make a well intentioned point.

Men calculate worth and value differently than God. In fact, this is what Jesus had to say about the "least of these":

> **"Whatever you've done to the least of these, you've done to me"**
>
> **– Matthew 25:40c**

That's right, Jesus – the King of kings and Lord of lords – esteemed Himself of no reputation by identifying as the "least of these." On the other hand, we use all manner of shallow and worldly calculations to measure people in a vain attempt to place us above someone else. Have you ever compared yourself to someone else whom you knew didn't measure up just to make yourself feel better in any of the following areas? Check off how many markers you've used to place your value above someone else:

- Education/intelligence
- Income level
- Beauty
- Body size
- Living location
- Religion
- Political affiliation

- Citizenship status
- Skin color/ethnicity
- Sexual purity/ orientation
- Marital status
- Children (bearing and rearing)

If we're honest, each of us has done this at some point in our lives but look at what Jesus had to say about such comparisons in Luke 16:15:

"You are the ones who declare yourselves just and upright before men, but God knows your hearts. For what is exalted and highly thought of among men is detestable and abhorrent (an abomination) in the sight of God."

God has a very different measuring device than men. His thoughts are not our thoughts and neither is His math our math when it comes to valuing individual worth.

I had a chance to go on a mission trip to Haiti in 2017. While I was there, the Lord expressed this truth to me during a church worship service. We were all worshipping together despite language barriers when suddenly, I sensed the strong presence of the Holy Spirit and began weeping. The song that the worship team was singing was in French and though I couldn't understand it, my spirit clearly understood what the Spirit of the Lord was communicating. He was saying that although Haiti appears to be despised as the least of these from the perspective of the world, Haiti is far from disposable. In fact, it is very valuable and precious in the eyes of God; as such, whoever blesses Haiti will be blessed by God. He expressed how much He loved the atmosphere of praise that was being created by the unity of the hearts of the Haitians and the Americans. God was pleased that we had taken time to associate equal value to a nation that is seen in His eyes as a treasure of His heart.

THE WEAKNESS OF THESE

Webster's Dictionary defines weakness as follows: **weakness: noun – lacking strength; deficient in physical vigor; feeble, debilitated; not able to resist external force or withstand attack; mentally or intellectually deficient; wavering, vacillating; not able to withstand temptation or persuasion; not factually grounded or logically presented as an argument; not able to function properly; lacking skill or proficiency; lacking normal intensity or potency; not having, or exerting authority or power; ineffective, impotent**

I'm not sure about you, but I'm not exactly excited to identify with the definition of weakness. Neither is society as we have a culture that celebrates the strong and prideful. We have a culture that's grounded in the competitive belief system of Darwin's theory of the "survival of the fittest." For all intents and purposes, we live in a culture that despises those who appear to be weak based on society's standards of strength. In fact, we go as far as to separate ourselves from the weak; effectively labeling them as the least amongst us. The problem with that perspective is that we all have "least of these" attributes within us. Are you in touch with the "least of these" attributes in you? More so than our strengths, the stories of our weaknesses and frailties connect us to each other. Until we're able to acknowledge our weaknesses, we will be unable to tap into the unseen connection that exists among us. In fact, by not doing so, we are choosing to defer to what separates us by default. Paul once stated that he would rather boast in his infirmities because it was from this position of humiliation that the grace of God empowered the purpose of his life which was to reconnect the Gentiles to God through Christ Jesus (see 2 Corinthians 12:5-10). On the opposite end of the spectrum, the fear of being weak keeps us rooted in the shameful illusion of separation. This fear of being seen as weak is what keeps us pointing the finger at the weakness of others.

This fear of being seen as weak keeps our powerful testimonies of victory (over weakness) trapped in our broken hearts; as we allow ourselves to be convinced that such transparency will only bring about our alienation. So what do we opt to do instead?

We wedge ourselves into the fittest – surviving through the pretense of perfectionism... all for the sake of a false sense of connection. Yet, if you've been paying attention, true connectedness comes from the realization of our common flaws relative to our uncommon God.

I can recall a time in my life when I felt particularly weak. Giving credence to the lies that I'm somehow stained as a Christian since I got a divorce and feeling guilty about the reports that divorce has become as common among Christian marriages as it is in non-Christian marriages. So imagine the weakness and shame I felt when I went through a divorce. Initially, I avoided talking about it as opposed to allowing it to be part of my testimony to minister to and empower others who may have felt the same way. During this time, I realized that I had judged divorce from a place of fear and I was simply attracting what I had judged as it states in Matthew 7:1-2 "Do not judge and criticize and condemn others, so that you may not be judged and criticized and condemned yourselves. For just as you judge and criticize and condemn others, you will be judged and criticized and condemned, and in accordance with the measure you use to deal out to others, it will be dealt out against you." (Amplified Version). This is the law of sowing and reaping being put into play. I believe that judging is a form of sowing or planting seeds and when we sow or plant, the harvest eventually comes up in some area of our lives to give us the opportunity to forgive and release the fear. Though

I am in no way advocating that anyone should be proud of divorce; I <u>am</u> advocating that we should refrain from judging it and use the trials of our brokenness to connect with others, which consequently, heals the shame. Being part of a body of believers seeking to graft others into our community, as we share testimonies of weakness, the connection of the body allows the Holy Spirit to move freely within it. And remember, it's the least of these that often have the ability to maintain balance in the body (think back to the pinky toe!).

We all have a choice when we come face to face with the least of these within ourselves. We can either turn a blind eye to or hide it or… we can meet it head on with courage as we embrace it as a tool to reconnect (with) others. Even King David – filled with lust in his own heart yet known as a man after God's own heart – asked the Lord to help him realize his weakness:

> **"Lord, make me to know my end and the measure of my days - what it is; let me know and realize how frail I am."**
>
> **– Psalm 39:4**

If Israel's greatest king wasn't afraid to face his weakness, why are you? Returning to 2 Corinthians 12:5-10, when Paul (the Gentile's greatest apostle) begged the Lord to remove the thorn from his flesh, the Lord's response illustrated how we should treat our frailties:

> **"My grace is enough for you; for my strength and power are made perfect and show themselves most effective in weakness."**
>
> **(2 Corinthians 12:9)**

Simply stated, our weaknesses allow the power of God to be revealed. Not convinced? Here's a second witness:

> **"But God chose those whom the world considers foolish to shame those who think they are wise, and God chose the puny and powerless to shame the high and mighty. He chose the lowly, the laughable in the world's eyes - nobodies so that he would shame the somebodies. For he chose what is regarded as insignificant to supersede what is regarded as prominent, so that there would be no place for prideful boasting in God's presence. For it is not from man that we draw our life but from God as we are being joined to Jesus, the**

Anointed One. And now he is our God-given wisdom, our virtue, or holiness and our redemption. And this fulfills what is written: If anyone boasts, let him only boast in all that the Lord has done."

– 1 Corinthians 1:27-31

(The Passion Translation)

RECONCILING ACTION

In closing out this chapter and transitioning to the subject matter of the Holy Spirit that is to come, reconciliation to God through Jesus is the answer to the cause of separation. Even as we have been described as lively stones in the temple of God (as a body of believers with Jesus Christ being the chief cornerstone AND head), there is no connection between stones without mortar. The Holy Spirit is the mortar which connects us – filling in the gaps of our weaknesses to bond us together for a project that is bigger than the sum of its individual parts. As such, I would ask you not only to consider the following but to revisit it after reading the next chapter:

- Ask the Holy Spirit to partner with you in identifying the "least of these" in you that you've attempted to hide or suppress. Repent and ask for forgiveness then invite the Holy Spirit to heal the shame. Begin to embrace and love that part of you.

- Ask the Holy Spirit to reveal a relationship or a group of people that you've judged as weak or inferior. Repent and ask for forgiveness then ask Him to show you His view of this person or group. Begin to embrace and love them.

- Ask the Holy Spirit for the next action item to put your faith at the next level.

THE SPIRITUAL CONNECTION

HOLY SPIRIT: THE COMFORTER AND SPIRIT OF TRUTH

n John 14:26, Jesus said the following about the Holy Spirit:

> "But the Comforter (Counselor, Helper, Intercessor, Advocate, Strengthener), the Holy Spirit, Whom the Father will send in my name (in my place, to represent me and act on my behalf), He will teach you all things. And He will cause you to recall (will remind you of, bring to your remembrance)

everything I have told you." (Amplified Version)

The Holy Spirit is both a real person and a gift to us from God the Father; sent by Jesus to teach and remind us of everything that's important to His Kingdom agenda. In John 16:7, Jesus said:

> "I am telling you nothing but the truth when I say it is profitable (good, expedient, advantageous) for you that I go away. Because if I do not go away, the Comforter will not come to you (into close fellowship with you); but if I go away, I will send Him to you (to be in close fellowship with you)." (Amplification added)

Jesus was emphasizing the importance of our connection with the Holy Spirit; even going as far as to imply it being more advantageous to connect with the unseen Holy Spirit than to continue in physical fellowship with Himself as His disciples had

done. Developing a relationship with the Holy Spirit requires one to make the decision to believe in and interact with an invisible realm via faith: the substance of things hoped for and evidence of things not seen (see Hebrews 11:1). It requires a willingness to partner with the mysterious "unseen" realm of God in a meaningful and intimate way. The Holy Spirit waits in anticipation for the day when we decide to acknowledge Him as real; developing one of the most powerful partnerships that can be afforded to a person. Those who have accepted Jesus as Lord have been gifted the Holy Spirit Who awaits within us to be unpackaged for maximum impact on our heart, mind, will, imagination and emotions.

I remember the moment I made the decision to acknowledge and befriend the Holy Spirit. My life began an amazing process of transformation whereby He granted more access to new levels of perspective, self-control, love, compassion, and the gifts of the Spirit and a completely untapped reservoir of power. As I gave the Holy Spirit more access to my soul, I learned His language which I've experienced as a quiet whisper. This communication developed an inner "knowing" which I consult and rely on for wisdom, advocacy, counsel, understanding, knowledge and revelation in my everyday life, relationships, ministry, and practice as a psychologist. This became especially important to me as I launched out as a business owner by faith. These tenets have enabled me to operate not only in my purpose but for my loved ones and for those who allow me to speak into their lives. The Holy Spirit is helping me write this book even now. He is a "Know-It-All" Who desires to reach out and partner with all believers to understand the language and ways of heaven while we're still here on earth.

But how does one develop a personal relationship with the Holy Spirit? There are several steps. First, decide that the Holy Spirit is a real person and begin to acknowledge Him as such. Second, begin to establish a relationship with the Holy Spirit and get to know Him like you would any other person with whom you desire to develop a connection. Learn His ways and how He communicates. Third, spend time interacting with Him by asking lots of open-ended questions, being still, and actually waiting for responses. Expect Him to answer in His quiet, subtle voice and He will! Fourth, begin journaling what He's saying and share it with others to test the words of Holy Spirit. Just as there are fake friends, there are fake spirits out there, too! This practice of testing the spirits is outlined accordingly in the Bible:

"Beloved, believe not every spirit, but try the spirits whether they are of God: because

many false prophets are gone out into the world. Hereby know the Spirit of God: Every spirit that confesses that Jesus Christ is come in the flesh is of God:"

– 1 John 4:1-2

CONNECTION BEGINS WITH A THOUGHT

"For who has known or understood the mind of the Lord so as to guide and instruct Him and give Him knowledge? But we have the mind of Christ and do hold the thoughts (feelings and purposes) of His heart"
– 1 Corinthians 2:16 (amplification added)

Did you know that as we think and imagine, we literally change some of the functions and structures of our brains? Scientists are even now beginning to suggest that our DNA can change shape according to our thoughts. And you thought Christianity was the only institution coming up with weird ideas! Don't forget – it has been documented that people who have a negative thought life have shorter life spans. In fact, according to the Institute of Heart Math, thinking about things that cause fear or anger cause DNA strands to become smaller while feelings of love do the exact opposite. Does that not sound like the shortening and extending of life at the genetic level?

Now that I've shared the (mad) science of the matter, allow me to share the spiritual equivalent. A psychiatrist by the name of Dr. Karl Lehman developed a process used to establish a live, interactive connection to Jesus for the purpose of emotional healing. Known as the Immanuel Approach. This powerful process began by using our memory as a tool to connect with Jesus. A person is prompted to remember a time they encountered Jesus. They are then told to focus on the memory with their imagination. While remembering this thought, the person is encouraged to express appreciation of Who Jesus was to them in the moment of the memory. They are then brought back to the present moment and are asked to locate how Jesus is presently with them and the living and interactive dialogue begins. From there, many have recorded experiencing a life-changing time of interaction with Jesus… and it all started with a memory which converted into a healing encounter.

This is an interesting approach for therapists as many therapists tend to have clients focus on traumatic memories to identify periods of isolation and fear which they connect to current feelings of despair and loneliness. Either way, the power of the mind is being accessed through remembrance. The ability to choose what we remember and how we remember it is a powerful weapon and can be utilized intentionally for healing since the brain can't tell the difference between what's being imagined or focused on vs. what's actually being experienced in the natural realm. This being said, an interesting point to consider is that we get the opportunity to decide where to place the most emphasis in any given moment: Are we going to put emphasis on the emotion of the memory based on what occurred in the memory or the attitude we express as we think back on memory. Inviting Jesus into traumatic memories helps to change the perspective of the memory from feeling scary and alone to feeling connected and empowered.

I myself have had several opportunities to experience The Immanuel Approach firsthand and I currently utilize this approach on a daily basis with clients and during ministry. During my first encounter with Immanuel, I sat down on a couch in Dr. Lehman's living room as 7 to 8 therapists watched and recorded. I remember feeling my heart beating rapidly and my arm pits sweating as the subconscious fear of being judged began to swell up. I didn't know what Jesus would choose to focus on during my session but I decided to yield to Him in this process and allow myself to be vulnerable. The Holy Spirit had been leading me on a journey to discover the importance of vulnerability – so this opportunity was just another place to step out by faith. One of the lessons I remember as a highlight during this episode which stretched my life was how Jesus Himself embraced being vulnerable by yielding to the crucifixion. This would prove to be a crucial component of my experience as Jesus took me on a beautiful and memorable journey of healing.

We (Jesus and I) visited areas of my heart that I thought had been healed; yet He showed me deeper layers of healing yet to be done. We ventured back to when my parents divorced (I was 13 years old) then continued through to my own divorce as an adult. We even revisited the death of my mother's physical body or should I say her transition to Glory from this earth. Although, we were reexamining wounded areas in my heart, it was a peaceful and pleasant walk. I shed tears and felt burdens being removed that I hadn't even known were there as I trusted and followed Christ. At the end of the session, the entire lot of therapists experienced what it felt like to have "God with us" (the meaning of Immanuel) as

He released angels, healing, and revelation for others in the group who attested to all that He had shared with me.

THINKING ABOUT GOD

According to Andrew Newberg's *How God Changes Your Brain*, simply thinking about God changes our brain in the following ways:

- Improved neural functioning

- circuit activation and deactivation

- the formation of new dendrites and synaptic connections

- increases sensitivity to subtle realms of experience

- perceptions and beliefs expand

In short, God becomes real on a neurological level based on the how significant He is in your life. Isaiah 26:3 affirms this:

"You will guard him and keep him in perfect and constant peace whose mind is stayed on you." (Amplified Version)

It must be stated that according to Newberg's research, merely thinking about God does not guarantee positive changes in our brain; having a negative concept of God can be detrimental. This is not just for the atheists among us. For example, if we think of God as authoritarian, or One Who is completely controlling, it will activate a part of our brain that stimulates fear and anger which primes the mind to tend towards rebellion. Whereas, seeing God as a loving Father activates a part of the brain that stimulates a mutual feeling of love. From here, empathy can develop for those who are hurt which only enhances our social awareness; making us more prone for conflict resolution which reduces harmful emotions such as fear and guilt. Proverbs 23:7 literally comes alive in this section of Newberg's book: "As a man thinks in his heart, so is he…"

According to another book, *The God Shaped Brain* by Timothy Jennings (2013), the greatest improvement from meditation occurred when people specifically meditated on God as love. The results of these thoughts included improvements in empathy, sympathy and compassion; which are all very integral when it comes to relationships. The notion is simple enough for believers and backed up with enough scientific data to prove it: when we think "rightly" on God's true nature, our love for others increases and our memory improves as our brains are stimulated to heal and grow.

5

TRUE IDENTITY

IDENTITY: WHO ARE YOU?

'd like to begin this chapter by unconventionally answering one of the greatest existential questions of all time: Who are you? My approach to the answer begins with Jesus, though. Beginning in Matthew 16:15, Jesus asked His disciples:

"But whom do ye say that I am?"

To which Simon Peter replied:

"Thou art the Christ, the Son of the living God."

Jesus then offered this powerful retort to conclude the matter: "Blessed art thou, Simon Barjona: for flesh and blood hath not revealed it unto thee, but my Father which is in heaven. And I say also unto thee, That thou art Peter, and upon this rock I will build my church; and the gates of hell shall not prevail against it."

I believe this exchange unveiled several powerful mysteries. The first being that we must receive a revelation of Who Jesus is in order to discover the revelation of who we are. All of mankind's identity and function can be discovered based off of the prophetic revelation of Who He is. Prophetic revelation, the release of a truth from heaven into the earth, is the foundation of being persuaded of Who Jesus is and who we are in Him. The second reveal is this: once we discover through revelation who we are, we can see the true identity of who others are in Christ.

When Simon Peter answered correctly, Jesus knew that he received it not from his carnal thoughts or those of his peers' but from heaven because we can't rightly know from our own mind Who Jesus is. The reason being that our carnal minds are in a state of enmity against God (see Romans 8:7).

Jesus went on to say that the church would be built on this revelation. Meaning, the foundation of the church would be built upon the same revelatory process which allows us to understand Who Christ is – faith to faith, brick by brick, and person by person. The church is to be erected on revelation from heaven which in turn, builds up its members by seeing each one from the perspective of heaven. Lastly, Jesus went on to offer the capstone of this building project in verse 19, stating to Peter:

> **"And I will give unto thee the keys of the kingdom of heaven: and whatsoever thou shalt bind on earth shall be bound in heaven: and whatsoever thou shalt loose on earth shall be loosed in heaven."**

Let's break down the three stages of this revelation process, shall we? It began with Peter receiving revelation from heaven about Who Jesus is, followed by continued revelation of who Peter was; accented by him receiving the keys to the kingdom of heaven. What's the point, you ask? Having a true revelation of Who Jesus is and who we are, grants us the ability to open and close doors for *others* to discover who they are relative to Jesus, as well. It's all connected (pun definitely intended)! The Kingdom of God is all about divine connections being established through heavenly revelations here on earth. I can hear your next question, though: How can we ever possibly apply this to our lives? It begins with a seemingly simple question and ends with waiting for a profoundly simple answer. An answer that could mean the beginning of your freedom: WHOSE are you?

The simple truth of the matter is this: we cannot connect with our Creator in a meaningful way if we don't know whose we are. Much like an earthly parent, knowing who we are relates to knowing Who our Father is; but before you can do that, you have to cast down some imaginations about who and what you thought yourself and God ought to be:

Who have you imagined yourself to be?

What have you imagined about yourself?

What have you imagined about God and others?

What roles have you attached your identity to?

I asked one person this set of questions and he answered the same way most people tend to formulaically respond:

"I'm a [fill in career here], a [fill in parent status here] and a [fill in spousal status here]."

When I asked him to strip away the roles and tell me who he was, he became confused and couldn't adjust his response. Then I asked him to be still and ask God. Within 30 seconds, he began weeping as he stated that God told him that he was a child of God. The answer was neither profound nor something that any of us haven't heard; but because he received it directly from the heart of God, it profoundly impacted his life. From that day on, he began living based on <u>who</u> he was as opposed to <u>what</u> he was doing. If I may, He began to see himself as a human "being" instead of a human "doing" – choosing to discover his purpose in life rather than doing what would garner the approval of others.

The reason we need to know who Jesus is before we can know who we are is because Genesis 1:26 tells us that we were created in His image. According to Merriam Webster, the word image means: **image: noun – a reproduction or imitation of a form of a person or thing, exact likeness, a tangible or visible representation of someone or something**

You, good reader, are the form of, exact likeness and tangible/visible representation of God! This is why the first part of Psalm 139:14 says that you were fearfully and wonderfully made! If only we could get the last part into our stubborn minds which says: "…and that my soul knows right well." We need to unlock (loose) such revelations from heaven and then lock (bind) it to our souls before we can expect to have a deep, meaningful connection with others. We need the revelation that identity is not what we do; rather, it's who we are.

Quite frankly, if we are merely what we do but never get the resources to do "the do," then by definition, we are nothing. Taking it a few levels deeper, If we attach our identity to what we do then technically, it's connected to the "dos and don'ts" of sin. With identities attached to sin, we will always be shamefully self-conscious about what disqualifies (separates) us from ever getting God's full revelation of who He intended us to be when He created us in His image and likeness. This is why Jesus' sacrifice is so crucial for us because in eliminating sin, He reestablished the ability to receive revelation from heaven about who you are and why you were created. Nothing on earth can correctly reveal that to you. In truth, when we are ignorant of such truth, we are kept in a darkness that glorifies the work of the devil which he began with Adam and Eve. In short, we don't have a behavior (what are you <u>doing</u>?) problem, we have an image (who are you <u>being</u>?) problem. We all behave according to the internal image that we've imagined for ourselves which has been skewed by the false revelation gained from the knowledge of good and evil. In other words, we're using knowledge from what others have said about us, what we think about ourselves and every other source outside of the revelation from Christ. As such, whatever we perceive to be on the inside gets projected to the outside with little to no effort.

THE REAL PERSON IS UNSEEN

"While we look not at the things which are seen, but at the things which are not seen: for the things which are seen are temporal; but the things which are not seen are eternal."

– 2 Corinthians 4:18

God's great justice for humankind is restoring us back to our original design. One of my client's had a powerful encounter to reinforce this justification process. One day while waiting to go to the hairdresser, she noticed a young man sitting in a car behind her. Although it initially struck her as odd, she didn't think much of it. That is, until she came out two hours later only to find the young man still sitting in the car. As she attempted to get into her vehicle, she heard "Give me your money!" as he held a gun to her back. Surprising herself, she nonchalantly responded by saying "Really? I only had enough money on me to get my hair done!" The real shock came when she turned to face the young man. When she looked at him, what she viewed was not from her natural sight but from heaven's perspective.

She immediately recognized that she had been given a glimpse of how God viewed him. She experienced a vision of the man attempting to rob her as a beautiful being made in God's image… and it showed in her face. It showed in her face so much so that, without saying a word, he released the gun from her body and walked away with tears in his eyes. They had connected on a higher plain – one where she could see what God saw despite what the young man was doing!

The unseen image of this man which was imprinted upon her heart overpowered what was happening in the natural. Was this a demonstration of two people "being" in God's image becoming more powerful than what one person was "doing" in the natural? Was this an example of what the opening scripture in this section meant when it stated not to focus on what we can see because it's temporal but instead, focus on what we can't see (with our natural eyes) which is eternal? If so, then this means that when these two viewpoints occurred at the same time, the eternal overpowered the temporal; making the latter disappear. I contend that there are such potential possibilities surrounding us; affording us the chance to choose what to make "real."

If you recall the "Observer Effect" from Chapter 2, the possibilities of the quantum realm come into reality based on when the observer views it. Would you agree that a person's beliefs can affect their vantage point? To me, that means that we can convert possibilities into realities – confirming that the mind can truly change matter. My client was given the opportunity to see the young man from an eternal perspective which changed his behavior in the moment and quite possibly, for the rest of his life. This evidence more than suggests that our observations can influence the people and environment around us – bringing the unseen world (the invisible heaven) into the seen world (the visible earth). In order to do so though, we must remember that we are eternal beings; which means the most relevant and significant part of us goes largely unseen while on earth.

Another personal example of bringing the "unseen" into the "seen" occurred in 2012 when one of my sister's (Dionne) was hospitalized and was fighting for her life. The doctors were confused about what was going on and in some ways, it still remains a mystery. However, she was in and out of consciousness and the doctors were speaking death over her and her life. While they were speaking death, I made sure to respond with life and to never allow death to be the last words spoken over her due to the power of words (see Proverbs 18:21) "The power of life and death are in the tongue". While I was sleeping one night, I had a dream from the invisible realm. I dreamt that my sister (Dionne) and I were walking and talking and she asked me if our mom knew that she was fine. My mom was living at the time of the dream, but in the dream, I said "no" she doesn't know. When I woke up from that dream my sister was still in the intensive care unit in the hospital fighting for her life and in and out of consciousness, but our merciful God, shared another possibility for her life with me and invited me to partner with the possibility in the invisible or "unseen" realm. The Holy Spirit invited me to only "see" my sister as she was in the dream or the "faith" realm, alive, healthy, and whole, which was completely contrary to what the doctors were saying and what we were seeing in the natural realm. I began focusing and meditating on that image and speaking it into being. For example, when the doctors would say things like, "it doesn't look like she'll make it and if she does, she won't walk again (she had drop foot from being in the bed for so long), I immediately and lovingly responded with a smile saying "my sister will live and she will walk again, we know and believe in Jesus and His resurrection power Often, those words were met with looks of pity and discouragement. ." I would also say to the doctors "You must be the best because I prayed that only the best would work on my sister". They would often smile at that compliment. Despite the doctor's negative expectations and reports, by the Grace of God, Dionne lived and is healthy and walking today...Praise God!! Even the hospital called it a miracle and didn't know how to explain it, but we know the explanation.

Let's make a conscious decision to stop focusing on the outside (temporal) and start concentrating on the inside (eternal). Once we realize that only false identities live via attachment to our physical bodies, we'll learn to embrace detaching ourselves from them; as we discover that "dying to self" is not death in our physical bodies but death (separation) from physical attachments to our bodies. As we learn to distinguish our true (eternal) nature from what can be physically seen, we'll begin to access who we've been redeemed to be in eternity through Jesus. As we are baptized in His death, so too are we baptized in His resurrected, eternal body (see Romans 6:3-4). When we've detached ourselves from what others see, we'll be better positioned to look further, deeper, and beyond into the everlasting life that we've been given access to – an everlasting life where signs, wonders, miracles and healings can occur in the here and now. Such acts are attributed to gifts of the Holy Spirit (see 1 Corinthians 12:7-11); however, we can't develop an intimate relationship with an unseen Holy Spirit while we're still so attached to our physical bodies. In essence, the less attached we are to the physical (temporal) realm, the more real the Holy Spirit can become.

IDENTITY AND THE HEART

The heart determines the course of our lives because the heart is where identity is stored. Who we believe ourselves to be is reinforced every time our heart beats as the message "This is who you are..." thumps your chest; solidifying what people come to know you by regarding your health, relationships and values. This is why true change occurs from the inside-out, not from the outside-in:

> **"Guard your heart above all else, for it determines the course of your life."**
> **– Proverbs 4:23 (New Living Translation)**

> **"Keep vigilant watch over your heart, that's where life starts."**
> **– Proverbs 4:23 (The Message Version)**

IDENTITY AND THE MIND

Beauty is in the mind of the beholder… yes – I know that's not how the saying goes but just go with it for a moment. One of the major points this book is meant to drive home that's of utmost importance to remember is that our identity is wrapped up in Christ. Everything that we are meant to be resides in; but how will we know what those things are on our own? Fortunately, we've already been given the answer:

> **"Now we have received, not the spirit of the world, but the spirit which is of God; that we might know the things that are freely given to us of God. Which things also we speak, not in the words which man's wisdom teaches, but which the Holy Ghost teaches; comparing spiritual things with spiritual. But the natural man cannot receive the things of the Spirit of God: for they are foolishness unto him: neither can he know them, because they are spiritually discerned. But he that is spiritual judges all things, yet he himself is judged of no man. For who hath known the**

mind of the Lord, that he may instruct him?
But we have the mind of Christ."
– 1 Corinthians 2:12-16 (emphasis added)

Therein lies the great reveal of our true identity: for <u>we</u> (those who confess Him as resurrected Lord and Savior) have the mind of Christ. David Benner (2004) reinforced this notion when he said:

"We find ourselves by finding God. If we find our true self, we find God and if we find God, we find our true selves."

Another way to look at this can be found in the Song of Songs TPT (also known as the Song of Solomon). Written by King Solomon as a letter to a Shulamite woman who had captured his heart, this canonized book of the Bible is full of romantic imagery. As viewed by her lover, this woman was truly transfigured in the eyes of her beholder, Solomon. The allegory that has been drawn over the years however, is that his view of her is how the Church and Bride of Christ is viewed by Her Groomsmen.

Hence, the allegory is about how Jesus views the community of Christian believers in His heavenly mind. Within the letter, Solomon expounded on the beauty of his love with phrases such as "You are so lovely..." and "You are so lovely, like the fine linen curtains of the Holy Place..." to affirm her. Being a woman myself, I know what it's like to see myself through the eyes of someone who has looked past my imperfections to see me – the real me – even when I'm incapable of doing so myself. The empowerment contained within such an exchange is a connection that can only be found in the heart of God. This experience is muddled at best when we've operated in carnal (physical, temporal) love but can receive the clarification it needs once we are seated in Christ. Once we are able to recall that we, being made in God's image, are meant to be a beautiful reflection of Him, we are then enabled to share this rediscovery with the world at large. Doing so combats what has happened far too often to many of us as we've been conditioned to look through a looking glass darkly:

> **"For now we see through a glass, darkly; but then face to face: now I know in part; but then shall I know even as also I am known."**
> **– 1 Corinthians 13:12**

> **"...He is like unto a man beholding his natural face in a glass: For he beholds himself,**

and goes his way, and straightway forgets
what manner of man he was."

– James 1:23b-24

the former passage of scripture is fitting as the entire context of 1 Corinthians 13 has come to be known as the chapter of love in the New Testament.

Returning to Song of Songs, it is important to note that the woman hadn't changed anything about her physical appearance; after all, how could she transform the locks of her hair into a flock of goats (see Song of Songs 6:5)?!! What the author attributed aspects of her esteem to were deemed as valuable and precious commodities in his culture. Such correlations can only be truly evaluated in a mind renewed by Christ:

"And be not conformed to this world: but
be ye transformed by the renewing of your
mind, that ye may prove what is that good,
and acceptable, and perfect, will of God."

– Romans 12:2

As the object of Solomon's affection, all she had to do was simply accept the accolades being credited to her so that she, too could be transformed by the renewing of her mind. Likewise, as we get revelation of who we are in the mind's eye of God, we should then become more charitable in how we view others. After all, just as "mind" and "heart" were interchangeable, "charity" and "love" were actually viewed as identical, as well. Hence, to discover who we are in God is simply not enough. We must then "give as we have received" to others around us – doing unto others as it has been done to us by affirming their true identity until they come into agreement with it.

THE MASTER SYSTEM

According to the book *Rare Leadership* by Marcus Warner and Jim Wilder, the brain has a master system that's in charge of building a healthy identity as a functionality of our mind. Within its pages, this book illustrated how brain scans have revealed that there's a pathway in each of our brains that starts at the bottom of the right hemisphere and works its way forward in four distinct stages. The stages correlate to joy levels. On the way to the forefront of our mind, the brain takes a picture of where the person is relative to their environment at a given moment; it then proceeds to a picture every 6 seconds. Warner and Wilder found that while resilient brains with high joy levels are able to progress through the cycle thus completing the pathway without interruption; the image of what they coined as "low joy" brains were not able to complete the path without several interruptions. The result? The image (of the person) became stuck as they transitioned through the landscapes of their world. This process confirmed the importance of having a healthy concept of who we are i.e. our identity.

For example, I had a client who struggled with an addiction to alcohol. Whenever she drank, she did so in excess which began to negatively impact her relationships; especially her relationship with her boyfriend. Rather than taking the "cold turkey" approach, we addressed this issue from the inside out. She wasn't happy with who she passively chose to be when she abused alcohol, so I asked her two questions:

- Who are you?

- Who do you choose to be?

Once she received a revelation of who she truly was, she decided to make the decision to become that person; effectively allowing the mental image she had of herself to complete its path through to "higher joy" levels. After that, she moved from the shame of what she'd been doing to the joy of who she was becoming: making drinking decisions that evolved from out of control drinking to moderate drinking or not drinking at all. Once she got a glimpse of this image and established it as her true identity, her mind began reinforcing this new identity with imagery every 6 seconds as it became far easier for her to change her mind and make better decisions. The final stage of her empowerment came when she was able to consistently think of herself from the standpoint of "This is who I am" versus "I can't drink." This new thinking completely transformed this client's life. She was able to drink moderately without abusing alcohol, her relationships improved significantly, she got engaged, she connected with her purpose, she obtained her dream job in the field that she loved and she was very happy.

THE FOUR STAGES

As alluded to in the previous section, according to Warner and Wilder in Rare leadership, the brain has four stages (or centers) that contribute to identity within the Master System that are worth illustrating:

LEVEL ONE: <u>The Attachment Center</u>: This stage is all about relationships. The greatest pleasure of the Attachment Center is joyful relationships. As such, it lights up CT (computed tomography) scans when we are around someone we like. When we reestablish a connection with God, this Attachment Center (if I can coin a phrase from our youth) stays LIT more than most!

LEVEL TWO: <u>The Assessment Center</u>: This stage is closely related to our "fight-or-flight-or freeze" response. We (rather, the image of ourselves) can get stuck here if there's unresolved trauma from situations that we perceived as dangerous from our past.

LEVEL THREE: <u>The Attunement Center</u>: This stage is where we attune; meaning we seek to acclimate to our environment by determining if anyone can relate to our circumstance(s). This is also called "mutual mind" – which is the state where we can bridge connections between our minds and others via the vehicle of our emotions. When we emotionally synchronize with others, we gain their perspective. Thus, this phase cultivates what we know as empathy. The Attunement Center is also where we connect with and gain the perspective of God; further evidence that we have been intellectually designed as relational beings.

Though traumas are recorded in LEVEL TWO and can disrupt how we view ourselves, they can actually affect LEVEL THREE's "mutual mind" – creating the illusion that we're alone in that there are no other minds with which to connect. This even has the power to minimize the strength of our memory; reinforcing our propensity to, as the integration of 1 Corinthians 13:12 and James 1:23-24 suggested, look through the glass darkly and forget straightaway what manner of wo/man we are. When we don't have mutual mind, the individual memory and emotions are magnified and the experience or trauma becomes far bigger than it really was.

LEVEL FOUR: The Identity Center: Lastly, this stage is self-explanatory. The more grounded the Identity Center is, the more emotional capacity we have to accept the identity of ourselves and others. Though we lose this as we get older, as infants, we graduated to this process early and often in our developmental stages. It has been documented that we actually have "mirror neurons" which are activated when we watch and emulate what someone else is doing; suggesting that we first begin grooming who we are at a subconscious level. Pairing such neurological pathways with the mind of Christ in others, the more we see Christ-centered activities around us, the more we will activate our renewed minds to become like Him and multiply His image on earth! This is why a Christ centered community is so important for the healing process.

THE ATTACK ON IDENTITY

This multiplicative property of Christ represents a threat to the prince of the power of the air and rulers of the darkness of this world. God knew this from the beginning which is why Adam received his mandate to be fruitful and multiply. It's no wonder then, that the enemy of God became the tempter of mankind when he attacked our identity by insulating the truth with a lie. From the beginning, the devil questioned whether or not we were made in the image of God:

"And the serpent said to the woman, You shall not surely die: For God knows that in the day you eat thereof, then your eyes shall be opened, and ye shall be as gods, knowing good and evil."

– Genesis 3:5

Our most powerful trait has always been that we are made in the image and likeness of God; hence, the serpent immediately took what seemed like a preposterous statement and planted a seed that mocks our origin story to this day. If you didn't know already, God is the ultimate strategist! His counterattack measure factored in Jesus – referenced as "the seed" – from the beginning (see Genesis 3:15). As such, when the Word of God showed up on the scene as the Son of God, we were provided with the perfect model to follow.

After Jesus had His identity established in Matthew 4:3, the devil (now being referenced as the "tempter") immediately yet fruitlessly went to work to attack it. Using the same old tactics from the Garden of Eden, satan once again insulated the truth with a lie by tempting Jesus to test His God status:

> **"...IF you are the Son of God, command these stones be made bread... IF you are the Son of God, cast yourself down: for it is written, He shall give his angels charge concerning you: and in their hands they shall bear you up on their hands, lest you dash your foot against a stone."**
>
> **– Matthew 4:3, 6 (emphasis added)**

With his subtle craftiness fully exposed, the devil attempted to use doubt and Jesus' hunger to beguile the Son of God; knowing that He had just finished a forty day fast (what IS it about the devil and food, by the way?... picking fruit from the tree, turning stones to bread, ice cream and devil's food cake...). Jesus wasn't having it, though. God spoke it, the devil tested it and Jesus (the Word of God) reinforced the truth. This is the school of thought for God and all of His would-be Kingdom citizens. When we renew our mind, make a decision or speak something that agrees with what God said about us, we can expect the tempter to test us. However, it's really our opportunity to reinforce the truth of what we already decided or spoke that confirms the truth of who we are. The tempter knows that if he's able to get us to question our true identity, he may be able to distract us or prevent us from fulfilling our purpose and destiny.

Think of it this way. When we're in school, we're given information to shape our knowledge and understanding of the concepts that were presented to us in school. The amount of information we're given from kindergarten through high school to successfully form us is actually staggering. To gauge our retention and apprehension of such material, we're given anything from quizzes and tests to comprehensive exams.

Failing to pass a test may delay us from moving onto the next level in school. Likewise, tests in life (though often created by the enemy to break our spirits but used by God to refortify them) serve as reminders of what we should already know:

"This is my beloved Son, in whom I am well pleased."

– Matthew 3:17

if we would just be attuned to the voice of God, we would discover that this basic truth is only the beginning of our restoration. Our identity in Christ is only the first step. So dust yourself off from your most recent attack and get ready to step into your eternal purpose!

SEEING OTHERS RIGHTLY: THE KEY TO BUILDING COMMUNITY IDENTITY

When I was in first grade, I struggled in school. Though my reading was pretty good, I just didn't get math. In fact, I was quite well known for not understanding math. I was unprolific! So much so, that I often had an audience around my desk admiring the errors on my math papers. Though there was only so much I could do to physically withdraw from a classroom designed for first graders, I retreated so far within myself that I felt as though I was watching from a distance as my peers marveled at how dumb I was. The shame of it all so greatly affected me and I wound up being held back in the first grade. Despite my setback, I remember my mother consistently telling me how intelligent I was. The powerful part is that she didn't just say it, I felt like she truly believed it, so I began to believe her. Even though I never received help from a personal tutor, I progressively improved in school. By the fifth grade, my confidence had recovered so well that I had even developed a reputation as a winner of classroom spelling bees. By middle school, my self-assurance increased to the point that I actually began to see myself as smart. It was at this juncture in time, that I set my mind towards obtaining a doctorate degree in psychology. In high school, I had come full circle with my old nemesis of math: I was taking pre-calculus. Only this time, I was proficient at it! By the end of my postsecondary career, I fulfilled my middle school declaration; attaining two graduate degrees in the process.

Among the various colleges I attended, my mother's accreditation was the most critical. My mother continued to express her support and validation from my earliest years as a first grade student and all through graduate school. So much that she began calling me doctor and introducing me to people as such, before I even started my doctoral program. Though never distracted from my goal to become a doctor of psychology, I remember feeling quite uncomfortable accepting this title from her prior to graduation; but I reluctantly adjusted to it. By the time I defended my dissertation in 2014, my mother had already become a master teacher in defending my identity as a doctor; just as God had defended the divine Sonship of Jesus: an earthly Man of no reputation aside from being the illegitimate son of a carpenter from Nazareth. That's the power of seeing the unseen. That's the power of believing and speaking God's view into the lives of others based on their potential instead of their current status. This is the key to unlocking the power of the Church against which the gates of hell shall not prevail; and I am eternally grateful to both my mother and father for revealing this to me throughout my life.

As grateful as I am, though – the true sign of gratitude is to pay it forward. During my 11-year experience as a school psychologist, I encountered students who struggled with a myriad of behavioral, emotional, addiction and academic issues. Prior to meeting them, a thick file filled with their offenses typically preceded them; giving me both the opportunity to read the file and prejudge them before they arrived.

As I initially observed myself and other staff in our ritualized prep work, I decided to ignore the cues from my peers. I decided to distinguish myself from my respected colleagues by choosing **NOT** to read the full history of the students prior to meeting them; rather, I decided to give them a fresh start by interacting with them based on God's perspective. I wanted to meet with each student and afford them the opportunity to tell me their story with no backstory preconceived of my own knowledge. I remember sharing with many of the students what God was showing me about them at our initial meeting before I knew them and many of them responded with puzzled and confused looks on their face that I could find such kind and positive words to say about them. Many of them even questioned how I could possibly see anything positive in them. Was it a risk to choose not to read the comprehensive file before meeting the students? Yes! However, we're called to uphold God's image – not condemn the behaviors of ourselves or others. Such a shift in thinking innately carries risk but when viewed correctly, it can be seen as a moment of faith.

You see, when we decide who someone is based on our preconceived notions or previous behavior, that's called prejudice. If that word wasn't enough to alert your societal sensibilities, let's take it up a notch. From a spiritual point of view, when we decide who someone is based on preconceived notions or previous behavior, that's satanic. In the twelfth chapter of Revelation, after identifying the serpent in the garden as satan and the devil, we're shown that one third of the angels of heaven fell with him (see verse 9). Verse 10 continues the narrative by giving the serpent another name: "accuser of the brethren." There, I've said it. Once you've allowed your preconceptions of a person to accuse and assume the worst of them, you have effectively taken the side of the devil. Let's rise above such small-mindedness. Let's ask how this person can be helped in correcting their image. Just as God called Abraham (meaning "father of many nations") out of Abram who had no children at the time and Gideon a "mighty man of valor" prior to him winning any battle, He's calling us to call others out based on His heavenly vantage; and trust me, He will readily share this vantage with those who ask.

THE TEMPTATION OF USING OUR NATURAL EYES TO SEE ONE ANOTHER

In all honesty, it is difficult getting out of the practice of seeing someone beyond their reputation; even if they've begun to make changes. In fact, this epidemic is so widespread in educational communities that there's a name for it: the Sustaining Expectation Effect (SEE). SEE is when teachers expect students to continue to achieve or behave according to previously established patterns to the point of ignoring evidence of change. Once a teacher has become so entrenched in his/her way of seeing a student, s/he responds through previous expectations instead of making the necessary adjustments. But teachers are not the only guilty party. Everyday civilians often do this in relationships; writing off any observable changes as short-term, chance, fake or even nonexistent; leaving the person who has changed in a futile position.

As if SEE wasn't enough, educational background is going to put a little more pressure on you! In the realm of neuroscience, there is something known as the Reticular Activating System (RAS). RAS provides the infrastructure connecting our brain to our spine and assists in mediating our overall level of consciousness. Basically, it helps us see what we already believe; therefore, it also hinders us from seeing anything that our belief system doesn't support. In other words, if we don't believe that someone can or has changed despite evidence to the contrary, our mind doesn't register the changed behavior(s) as true.

This is the basic building block of stereotypes. This is also quite dangerous. When we develop negative beliefs about individuals or groups, our brains are neurologically wired to only support the evidence of what we already believe. The rest is simply disposed. But there is hope. By interrupting the "seeing cycle," we can influence the destiny of others. Without these interruptions, we can wind up perpetuating false beliefs into ourselves and others that ultimately pigeonhole the mind into an extremely narrow view of the world and its inhabitants. If you're narrow-minded in any area of your life, choose to repent (change your mind) of the way you've been seeing the world. Instead, opt to give people a clean slate; not with a benefit of the doubt but with the benefit of the faith. As you commit to doing this, watch what God does in yours and their hearts. He is truly a Restorer of the breach to those who believe. At the end of the day, the work that God does through how you choose to accept such response-ability allows others to see the unseen Father even as Jesus stated in John 14:9-12:

> **"Jesus said to him, Have I been with you so long, and yet you don't know me, Philip? He that has seen me has seen the Father; and how do you then say, Show us the Father?**

Don't you believe that I am in the Father, and the Father in me? The words that I speak unto you I speak not of myself: but the Father that dwells in me, He does the works. Believe me that I am in the Father, and the Father in me: or else believe me for the very works' sake. Verily, verily, I say unto you, He that believeth on me, the works that I do shall he do also; and greater works than these shall he do; because I go unto my Father."

THE WAY TO PEACE IS TO TRAVEL LIGHTLY

If I may, I'd like to spend some more time exploring the Attachment Center. To being, I'd like to quote from Dr. Eben Alexander's book *Proof of Heaven: A Neurosurgeon's Journey into the Afterlife*. In it, he wrote:

"The penetration of the higher worlds, tends to be a gradual process and requires the individual to release his or her attachments to whatever level he or she is on before going deeper."

I'd like to say that it started on a deep, spiritual journey but alas, it began in 2013 with a clogged ear, of all things! After the issue persisted, I made an appointment to go to the doctor to have my ear checked. Before I go any further, this must be said: I do believe that there's often a spiritual message for just about everything in the natural, so I asked God to reveal if there was something that He wanted me to hear that I wasn't hearing. As such, when I couldn't get the doctor I intended on seeing due to scheduling conflicts, I opted to make the appointment with a different doctor since it started becoming obvious to me that God was up to something. During my appointment, the doctor began telling me about a long-term mission's trip that he and his wife were preparing to take. Though I wasn't open to long-term, I immediately knew that God was opening my ears (and heart, for that matter) to a mission's trip. That entire situation occurred in the early part of the summer of 2013.

On July 18th, I met a friend for lunch who casually mentioned that there was a "watering hole meeting" that she had previously attended and enjoyed, however, she would have to miss going the next day, due to having to work. She suggested that I attend the meeting. It just so happened that I was going to be off that day and I was sensing a nudge from Holy Spirit to attend. My decision was immediate. On July 19th, I went and listened to a man named Larry Staker speak about China. As he spoke, I could feel God stirring up a small desire in my heart for China. After listening to him speak, I went through a "fire tunnel": where people stood on either side of a line as they prophetically prayed over the people who traversed through the prayer tunnel. When I got to one particular gentleman, he began to repeat one very powerful and scary word that immediately increased my body temperature and raised my heart rate as he stoked what God had stirred within me:

"Change, Change, and CHANGE!"

Each time he said it, I felt the intensity of my heartbeat drastically increase as my mind became more enthralled at the thought of what kind of change he could be talking about and when would this change occur? I was afraid of what it all could mean. As I continued working my way through the "fire tunnel", a powerful woman of God asked just as matter-of-factly:

"Are you supposed to go on a mission trip?"

I responded in the affirmative with unsure surprise. It had all happened so fast! I couldn't piece it all together to hear the message clearly at first. Where was I supposed to go, again? It wasn't until I was on the way home, that God began ministering to my heart about me going on a mission trip to China.

Four days later on July 23rd, I had a dream about my workplace. Within the dream, a friend of mine warned me that the school was getting rid of "certain types of teachers … (those who had worked at the school the longest" and that it was time to go!" I remember waking up at that moment then falling back to sleep. The dream seemingly picked back up where it had left off; only now, I was telling my sister, Pauline about my dream while still in the dream. She interrupted me before I could finish to tell me that her son – my nephew Luke – had a dream where he was telling people about how his Aunt Lisa worked in schools but that the schools were moving teachers out into garages. I began crying in my dream as I finished telling it to Pauline because I knew what it all meant: It was time for a transition from my workplace. I needed to prepare. A change was coming. It was a bit emotional because although it was being revealed to me that my season at my job was coming to an end, I still enjoyed what I was doing and I was on good terms with my workplace.

On July 25th, another friend of mine named Renee called me out of the blue to inform and invite me on a journey out of the country to… you guessed it: China! I couldn't believe it! She had confirmed what God had been revealing to me since this course began with my ear being clogged yet, it all seemed so fast! Though the trip that Renee mentioned was only a tour of China (not a literal missions trip), she made her intentions clear to me that she would be praying for people along the way. There was only one layered problem. My sister (along with my twin nephews) had just moved in with me from Arizona after filing for divorce from her husband. She and my nephews were still in a lot of pain so I felt like I needed to be there for them. Did I mention that my mother was also living with me at the time? This added another dynamic as I felt like the one responsible for bringing balance in a house where two matriarchs (my oldest sister and mother) had been challenged in keeping peace with one another. As if the duty of being a sister and daughter to two matriarchs under one roof wasn't enough to leave unsupervised, one of my nephews begged me not to go; making it all the more difficult for me as the thought of my leaving had even driven him to tears and consequently, brought tears to my eyes.

To make matters more inconvenient, I had been off from work for several weeks during the summer. This trip (which I found out would be seventeen days) was scheduled for early September, which would end up being shortly after the new school year began. How could I go back to work and ask for seventeen days off at the most critical time of the year after just having a big portion of the summer off? Seventeen days not only felt like a long-term mission's trip but a long time to be away from home, in general. The timing felt completely off, so naturally, I began to pull back a little. Despite all the turn of events and confirmations in the form of prophetic prayer and direct counsel from God I'd received, I still needed to pray and speak to friends. I wrestled for several weeks – contemplating and resisting the opportunity that God had created for me and planted in my heart. Though I had heard the call as clear as day, it was at this point in time that I realized I was too attached.

Upon this realization, I made the decision that I was going to list and let go of my attachments with the help of the Holy Spirit:

- I was attached to my family

- I was attached to having things my way

- I was attached to my job

- I was attached to my routine and predictable schedule

- I was attached to the approval of man

I decided to yield to the Holy Spirit. I decided that I was going to trust God and (let) go. I chose to accept the invitation of the Holy Spirit to go to China. This was definitely a higher level of faith I was beginning to operate in – accentuated by the fact that I purchased my ticket <u>before</u> telling my work boss to help me to let go of any attachment to approval from man and idolatry of my job that I may have had. I was convinced that a seventeen-day absence at the beginning of the academic year coupled with my long summer vacation was going to be the way that I lost my job. To my surprise, it wasn't. I was not only given the school's blessing to go; I was also given a promise that my position would be waiting for me upon my return. The moment I yielded to the Holy Spirit, let go of my control and acted on my newfound freedom, I also found peace.

Agreeing to China by temporarily letting go of a few attachments was just the first step. The entire experience allowed me to continue the process of letting go of attachments in my heart that were weighing me down. If you've ever traveled internationally, you know that one of the biggest challenges is learning how to travel lightly. Southwest or not, it's hard being free to move about the country when you've got too much baggage! I remember when I was on the plane waiting for everyone to board and for the plane to take off for China, I received a phone call from my earthly father, giving me the same message that my Heavenly Father had been giving me...he said "go and have a good time, leave Chicago and everything there behind". He was basically encouraging me to "let go", which I truly needed to hear even at that moment. While I was in China, God continued to unload my distractions as I connected and worshipped with Him daily despite the unpredictability of being in a new culture and swapping out where we would sleep. During my trip, since I didn't have access to the phone and contacting family and friends in the states, God became my circle of friends and family when I felt discomforted about how inaccessible I was to my circle of friends and family back home. Though designed as a tour, this excursion transformed into a mission's trip for God to my heart which humbled me in many ways. Through this process, He showed me that suffering occurs when we resist letting go of things, people and relationships i.e. life, as we know it. Suffering stems from a refusal to accept change when the opportunity presents itself. I struggled before I made my final decision to go because my heart resisted giving up the attachments with which I had become too familiar.

THE BENEFITS OF LETTING GO

Letting go is the beginning of every faith-based blessing. We must always be prepared to let go of something that we've been holding onto in order to receive that which God wants to replace it. Just envision clutching something in your hands. It is impossible to receive anything greater in your grasp until you release what's in your hand. That said, what's in your hand:

Physically?   Financially?

Emotionally?   Spiritually?

If you've ever tended a garden, you know there's no way to get fruits and vegetables if you never release the seeds from your hand into the ground. When investing to increase your finances, one must be willing to let go of a <u>portion</u> of what you already possess. When seeking peace in relationships, one must be willing to let go of past hurts and offenses (through forgiveness). To be healed from grief, we must be willing to let go of the life, experiences, or future that we had hoped to experience to make room for God to replace the void.

For example, when my mother went to be with Jesus, I had to make the decision to let go of the beautiful relationship that

I had with her while she was here and of my hopes about the role that she may have continued to play in my life if she had still been here. I chose to be grateful that I was blessed to have a mother that many never experience and to have her here on earth with us as long as we were blessed with her presence. I was blessed that my mother was present to share most of my life milestones before she transitioned. Another example was one of my clients came to me after losing her husband because she was still grieving him a year after he had passed away. She thought the pain was related to not being able to say goodbye to him before he passed though they knew that he was dying. Although that was part of it, the real pain was not being able to let go of the life she had with him, life as she knew it and the life she had planned to spend with him. This meant that she could not grasp the new life that God was forming for her. Once I asked her to specify which of the two the greater source of her pain was, she immediately had an epiphany that allowed her to identify her inability to release the life they had together as the source of pain. To wit, this was even the logic behind why she hadn't said goodbye to him; as she had thought that somehow, if she could avoid saying goodbye, he might not leave. Peace found my client once she received the revelation that the real issue was choosing to not let go.

If God is inviting you to higher levels of faith, we must first face the instances in the past where we feel as though He wasn't there for us...and release ourselves from the disappointment. When God invited me to let go of my job, I had to be willing to let go of the comfort and security of a regular paycheck beneath a glass ceiling in exchange for an infinite ceiling. I had to let go of the comfortable familiarity of my daily responsibilities in exchange for the freedom of uncertainty. In order to be led by the Comforter (Holy Spirit), I had to step out of my comfort zone as an act of faith.

What attachments are holding you back from living the life that God has for you? Is it attachment to your way of doing/thinking about things? Are you attached to your own expectation of how your marriage or spouse should be? Are you facing disappointment because of not being able to surrender those expectations and open your heart to what God wants to do? Are your struggling with attachments to unreasonable expectations of how your career or children were supposed to turn out? Are you attached to trying to stay young, or expectations of how your finances were supposed to be at your current age? Are you attached to how people groups (church, political parties, gender, nations) are supposed to be? Are you attached to a substance that you think you need to get through life? Are you attached to an emotion (anger, un-forgiveness, sadness, jealousy, anxiety, etc.) that you've been turning to in times of disappointment?

These attachments are taking up God's space! He wants to take the place of every attachment you think you need. He can do an infinitely better job of satisfying the voids in your life than any attachment you've been holding on to for dear life. If you are willing to allow the Holy Spirit to assist you in identifying the attachments that are hindering your relationship with God and others, please pray this prayer with me and watch these attached burdens fall to the ground as God is ushered in:

"Heavenly Father, In the Name of Jesus Christ, I confess, repent, and renounce the fear of "letting go" and holding onto people, places, and things and putting them before you or what you're inviting me to do. From this day forward, I'm choosing to release and let go of….(list everything that you're choosing to let go of) Holy Spirit, please take these things, empty me of this clutter that I have released and fill me up with your love, kindness, compassion, peace, forgiveness, gentleness, etc.

CHAPTER 6

FORGING AHEAD WITH FORGIVENESS

FORGIVENESS AND UNFORGIVENESS: TWO OF THE MOST POWERFUL PRINCIPLES OPERATING IN GOD'S KINGDOM

What if the only reason we're here is to perfect our love by walking in perfect forgiveness towards self and others?

In the previous chapter, forgiveness was alluded to as a way to release yourself from emotional attachments. Since the subject of forgiveness (and the lack thereof) has run so rampant in the lives of so many people, it only makes sense to dedicate an entire chapter to the matter. In the Gospel of

Matthew, unforgiveness is linked to emotional tormentors through the telling of the parable of the unforgiving servant (see Matthew 18:21-35). Emotional torment specifically related to unforgiveness is a spiritual doorway for cancerous manifestations in the body. While the world is searching for ways to stay healthy and keep the physical body alive, the church has held the key for a millennia:

"Beloved, I pray that you may prosper in every way and that your body may keep well, even as your soul keeps well and prospers."
– 3 John 1:2

The link is clear here: the key to keeping our bodies well is to make sure that our unseen soul is prospering. While the medical and psychological fields of this world are looking for ways to treat or medicate what they can see, the church has known all along that destroying the works of the devil (sickness, disease and affliction) is about healing what we can't see. Rather, the answer has been within arm's reach of the church; the problem is that the arms have atrophied by reason of un-use.

Although forgiveness and unforgiveness are unseen as spiritual principles, the effects of unforgiveness have ransacked the visible world. Wars, hatred, violence, murder, suicide, division, fear, anger, anxiety, depression – these are the results of unresolved bitterness and resentment; rooted in the offense-riddled chambers of hearts beaten by unforgiveness:

"Many will be offended and repelled and will begin to distrust and desert and will stumble and fall away and betray one another and pursue one another with hatred. And many false prophets will rise up and deceive and lead many into error. And the love of the great body of people will grow cold because of the multiplied lawlessness and iniquity."

– Matthew 24:10-12

simply stated, the accumulation of bitterness has warped our society into a cold version of what it's meant to be. And much like frostbite, such coldness must first be exposed before it can be healed and if necessary, cut off (unattached).

That said, our society seems determined to fix internal issues like unforgiveness through external measures via the brute force of carnal weapons (wars, weapons, surgery, medication, etc.); when in fact, internal strongholds can only truly be healed with the divine weapons of God:

"For though we walk in the flesh, we are not carrying on our warfare according to the flesh and using mere human weapons. For the weapons of our warfare are not physical, but they are mighty before God for the overthrow and destruction of strongholds, we refute arguments and theories and reasoning and every proud and lofty thing that sets itself up against the true knowledge of God; and we lead every thought and purpose away captive into the obedience of Christ."

– 2 Corinthians 10:3-5 (Amplified Version)

In other words, although we can see and experience the battle through our physical body, our method of attack is not to respond in kind. Rather, we are to respond by tearing down the intangible

forces with intangible yet mighty weaponry. This means war – and fighting natural fire with Holy fire is the way to win. This may seem trite but the best armament to disarm our enemy is through an "opposites attack" tactic as seen in in Luke 6:28:

"Bless those who curse you, pray for those who abuse you."

Blessings overcome curses. Love overcomes hate. Kindness overcomes cruelty. Patience overcomes impatience. Generosity overcomes greed. Diligence overcomes laziness. Joy overcomes sorrow. Forgiveness overcomes unforgiveness.

The thing is, we can't do any of these without first forgiving. Our worldly minds may have arguments, theories, opinions, and reasoning that attempt to persuade us to use worldly weapons to retaliate and protect ourselves; but surrendering to God's way of doing things is the key to real victory. The world's methods, as powerful as they may be to temporarily change the realm we see, garner false senses of triumph that are ethereal in the unseen realm where our eternity resides. In John 14:30, Jesus said:

"I will not speak with you much longer, for the ruler of the world is coming and he has no power over me, nor anything that he can use against me."

I believe the advantage that Jesus maintained in order to diffuse the power that the ruler of the world (the devil) had was largely based in His ability to forgive. You see, unforgiveness gives us something in common with the (false) ruler of the world. The way to eliminate such commonality is to maintain a willingness to forgive. The key to destroying the works of the devil, stripping the territory he's usurped from him and reconciling everything to Christ, is to no longer count people's sins against them once you've been forgiven of your own sins. Let's make a habit of going through life stripping satan of everything that he thinks he owns in this realm by releasing and forgiving ourselves and everyone else.

FORGIVENESS IS A DECISION TO AGREE WITH HEAVEN

If unforgiveness creates a commonality between us and the devil, then mustn't forgiveness create a commonality between us and God: the Father of heaven and earth?:

> **"This day I call the heavens and the earth as witnesses against you that I have set before your life and death, blessings and curses. Now choose life, so that you and your children may live and that you may love the Lord your God, listen to his voice, and hold fast**

to Him. For the Lord is your life, and he will give you many years in the land he swore to give your fathers, Abraham, Isaac and Jacob?"

– Deuteronomy 30:19-20

this scripture reinforced the fact that we're faced with decisions that lead to life and death for us and our descendants every day. I believe that forgiveness is one of these decisions. Forgiveness is a command and the Bible tells us that if we love God, we will obey His commands. When we obey His commands, we will be blessed. Contrarily, if we disobey His command of forgiveness and choose unforgiveness (intentionally or otherwise), we are subjected to a curse of torment. In God's Kingdom, obedience has nothing to do with feelings, but with covenant. This word was not chosen haphazardly. When we think of covenant, we tend to think (aside from "New" and "Old" associations to the Bible) of marriage. Married couples founded in Christ do not last based on love as a mere feeling; rather, they are sustained when love is acted out as a decision to honor and obey the covenant which God implemented as the institution of marriage itself. We may have chosen to love someone based upon an initial feeling but there will come a time when we won't always feel the same towards our spouse.

Feelings are temperamental; meaning, they are liable to change throughout a given day, no less a lifetime spent with someone. As such, if we make decisions based on our feelings alone, we will live an unstable and tormented life. The same is true with forgiveness. Many times, we may not *feel* like forgiving someone who has hurt us – especially if we believe that their actions were intentional. Our feelings, which are attached to our flesh, often scream for earthly vengeance. Coupled with our egos, feelings drive us with a need to see the perpetrator of our pain experience equal or even greater hurt as a form of self-serving retribution. This is not the justice of God. Even so, we often desire to take the gavel of justice from God in favor of executing [justice] ourselves.

"Repay no one evil for evil, but take thought for what is honest and proper and noble in the sight of everyone. If possible, as far as it depends on you, live at peace with every-one. Beloved, never avenge yourselves, but leave the way open for God's wrath; for it is written, Vengeance is Mine, I will repay says

the Lord. But if your enemy is hungry, feed him; if he is thirsty, give him drink; for by so doing you will heap burning coals upon his head. Do not let yourself be overcome by evil, but overcome evil with good."

– Romans 12:17-21 (amplification added)

Though He had access to such vengeance as God in Spirit, while on earth as a man, Jesus demonstrated forgiveness as a choice that we should yield to even when we don't feel like it. He not only taught it in His ministry but showcased the extreme lengths He was willing to go when He yielded to the plan of salvation that God the Father had for mankind which culminated with His physical death. This is supremely illustrated in Luke 22:42's retelling of His final hours before being arrested in the Garden of Gethsemane:

"Father, if you are willing, take this cup from me; yet not my will, but yours be done."

After acknowledging that the "cup" of God's wrath and judgment would be painful and cause suffering that He didn't want to go through, He yielded His will to God because He trusted the covenant of God's Will beyond the comfort of

His own. I believe that this depiction of Jesus being fully man, helps us to identify with the struggle that we will have in our flesh on this earth when it comes to parting from our flesh and obeying God. When executed as a choice within a covenant, forgiveness allows us to detach ourselves from the hurt, trauma, and pain attached to the memories of what we've identified as unforgiveable acts. I often like to use the metaphor of unforgiveness existing as a huge garbage bag filled with dreadful, heavy and putrid trash from a vice of vengeance-seeking. After accumulating such venom for a lifetime, the bag can begin to leak and break, wreaking havoc from such a reeking habit. To avoid being covered with the stench of its contents and the litter of the content into all areas of your life… just release the bag! As a side note, forgiveness does not condone the behavior of the offender; it pardons the offender. Such a pardoning act releases your heart (and even the other person's heart) from remaining captive to the bondage of pain and hurt.

The Medical and Emotional Benefits of Forgiveness: Connecting Forgiveness to Healing

During Jesus' earthly visitation, He announced the start of His ministry by quoting a familiar passage from Isaiah 61. However, when He got to the section which spoke about "opening the prison to them that are bound," He chose to use different language:

> **"...to set at liberty them that are bruised."**
>
> **– Luke 4:18e**

That word "bruised" implied a physical mark which, when you think of metal shackles being placed on a prisoner, makes sense. However, Jesus is King of a spiritual Kingdom. Hence, He spoke largely of freeing those bound in spiritual shackles; and unforgiveness bears the chains of the sturdiest mettle. Jesus' redemptive work on the Cross was often a package deal. In the same manner that we refer to insurance gained from employment as a "benefits package" – forgiveness of sins is part and parcel with physical and emotional healing. Observe Jesus' words spoken to the paralytic in Matthew 9:2:

> **"Take courage, son; your sins are forgiven and the penalty remitted."**

He continued in the verses that followed, speaking to the scribes and Pharisees who refuted His action:

> **"For which is easier: to say, your sins are forgiven and the penalty remitted, or to say, Get up and walk?"**

In this passage, Jesus announced forgiveness of sins as a part of the process that would ultimately heal a paralytic! Although Jesus didn't specify that it was the man's unforgiveness that caused his paralysis, it was clear that receiving forgiveness for his sins healed him. Going back to the book of Isaiah which prophesied of the coming Messiah and His mission, chapter 53 clarified this connection between the sins that He would address as the root of emotional and physical suffering, not the symptom. Simply put, sin is the causal issue, everything else is a secondary effect.

Despite being seen as unrooted in support of scriptures, science and medical research have found that there are many emotional and physical benefits to forgiveness. For example, according to Karen Swartz, M.D. (2014), director of the

Mood Disorders Adult Consultation Clinic at Johns Hopkins, forgiveness leads to decreased stress and anger; while not forgiving is associated with increased levels of unrestrained anger and sadness. Another study done in the Journal of Psychological Science (2001) found that when people held onto a grudge, they had more negative physiological activity including more facial muscle tension, increased heart rate, higher blood pressure and sweating; all of which abated with the release of long-held grudges.

Yet another study done in the Journal of Personal Relationships (2011), found that with married couples, when the target of an indiscretion forgave the committer of said discretion, <u>both</u> experienced a decrease in blood pressure.

SETTING CAPTIVES FREE

"The Spirit of the Lord is upon Me, because he has anointed Me to preach the good news to the poor; He has sent Me to announce release to the captives and recovery of sight to the blind, to send forth as delivered those who are oppressed. To proclaim the accepted and acceptable year of the Lord."

Bringing the fullness of Jesus' proclamation from Luke 4:18 back into focus, an essential key of Christ's ministry was setting captives free. Unforgiveness is a form of imprisonment that we are not inclined to see. Oftentimes, the people who I've led through forgiveness were too close to the emotionality of the offense to see their release being contingent upon the degree to which they were willing to forgive. From professional experience, a person's vision of their chains increases immediately upon unlocking themselves from their bondage with a key that had been in their hand the entire time. Such moments of clarity can be life changing. Here are some of the expressions I've heard from clients that completed the forgiving process:

In one of my most extreme cases of release, one client exclaimed the following after forgiving and releasing her deceased mother from what had once been an unpardonable offense:

"She's gone, she's gone, she's gone!" The moment this client forgave and released her mother, she realized that even though her mother had transitioned, she was carrying her mother with her by holding onto the painful and traumatic memories from when her mother was alive. She didn't realize the burden that she was holding onto until she walked through the forgiveness process and exchanged the heaviness for lightness. This caused her reaction of she's gone! She's gone! She's gone!

In yet another mother-client relationship afflicted by un-forgiveness the patient said with a smile regarding the stunted relationship she had with her live-in mother:

"We can have a relationship, I'm going to have a good relationship with my mom."

In keeping with the parent trend (longstanding relation-ships such as the ones we foster with our parents often have the heaviest fetters), another client stopped in the middle of the process and said:

"I just realized why I've always felt so much guilt and shame even when I didn't do anything wrong."

Recalling the parable of the unforgiving servant which was alluded to at the onset of this chapter, the servant's main issue was that he could not see the relationship between the large debt he was forgiven and the substantially smaller debt he failed to forgive of a fellow servant. He could neither see the correlation nor the consequence of his actions because of another essential principle Jesus explained in Matthew 7:3-5:

"And why do you behold the mote (speck) that is in your brother's eye, but you do not

consider the beam that is in your own eye? Or how will you say to your brother, Let me pull out the mote out of thine eye; and, behold, a beam is in your own eye? you hypocrite, first cast out the beam out of your own eye; and then you will see clearly to cast out the mote out of your brother's eye." (amplification added)

We're the same way. We're all one-sided spectators to forgiveness; ready to receive but incapable of seeing the preservation of our cleared debt as it's related to the pennies of penance we withhold from others. We can't have it both ways. We can't expect patience and compassion for our sin debt while arranging how we'll get revenge for someone else who's trespassed against us. We'd rather focus on demanding payment in the form of an apology or changed behavior; unaware that in putting our hands out for retribution, we are also placing our wrists into handcuffs. Worse still, we often become accustomed to our detainment; with preference given to our torturous arrangement. That's called Stockholm Syndrome, people. That's colluding with your captor while fending off your Savior: Jesus Christ. Doing so does not proliferate oneness with God. Doing so roots the illusion of separation into the physical world.

If a person did something to me that's so egregious that I can't forgive them, it's saying one or two things about me:

1) It's either saying that they're not like me because I'm incapable of committing something so reprehensible or...

2) It's saying that I know I've done some egregious things in my life that I'm...

    a. ashamed to even admit and/or...

    b. not worthy to be forgiven of; in turn, neither are they

Either way, it would be easier to do what the Lord's Prayer calls us to do, which is to forgive others' debts/trespasses so that we can be forgiven. Forgiveness frees us and our memories from the bondage of separation. Through reconnecting us to our Creator, forgiveness heals the emotional memories, physical body, soul and the spirit. Forgiveness releases us from the fear of eternal judgment, which is an underlying fear of many whether they believe in God or not. Forgiveness gives us permission to let go of poisonous memories – thus permitting us to live in the present.

As I conclude this section, I'd like to encourage you with yet another important concept. Sharing forgiveness as a testimony of something you've done is the most powerful aspect of experiencing the full range of this beautiful gift. It's the difference between it being a concept and living principle. Corrie Ten Boom is the author of *The Hiding Place*: a Christian who modeled the power of giving away forgiveness to someone who, by all measures (including their own) didn't deserve it. Corrie Ten Boom wrote and spoke about her family's experiences from hiding Jews from the Nazis in their home during World War II. They were eventually discovered and sent to a concentration camp where all of her family members died. Despite this, Corrie lived her life by sharing the power of God's forgiveness for the people who murdered millions of people, including her family. During one of her speaking engagements, she had an encounter with one of the men whom she described as the cruelest of the camp guards. He approached her after her speech and, with his hand extended, gave the following statement:

"Thank you for your fine message, how wonderful it is to know that all our sins are at the bottom of the sea!"

As she looked at this man in utter shock that he was actually the one responsible for the death of several of her family members, she considered what it all meant, she was faced with the decision to do exactly what she had been teaching. Although she paused, she eventually chose to give the gift of forgiveness as she extended her hand to the man who had caused so many painful memories. I'm confident that her decision to shake his hand planted a seed of the power of God in his heart as well as the hearts of those who witnessed it.

THE MINISTRY OF RECONCILIATION

The Corrie Ten Boom story and many stories in the Bible demonstrated how the ministry of reconciliation is supposed to operate.

"This means that anyone who belongs to Christ has become a new person. The old life is gone; a new life has begun! And all of this is a gift from God, who brought us back to himself through Christ. And God has given us this task of reconciling people to him. For God was in Christ, reconciling the world to himself, no longer counting people's sins against them. And he gave us this wonderful message of reconciliation. So we are Christ's ambassadors; God is making his appeal through us. We speak for Christ when we plead, 'Come back to God!' For God made Christ, who never sinned, to be the offering for our sin, so that we could be made right with God through Christ."

– 2 Corinthians 5:17-21

(New Living Translation Version)

The ministry of reconciliation is an extension of the ministry of forgiveness because forgiveness is what reconciles us back to God through Christ. Unforgiveness, on the other hand, is what keeps us divided (unreconciled). Further still, after reconciling us to God, the anointing of Christ remains on Christians that we might be reconciled one to another for the sake of destroying the consequences of being unforgiven. In and of itself, the definition of "reconcile" alludes to relational forgiveness:

reconcile: verb – to restore friendship, harmony or communion; adjust, settle

differences; to make congruous (an ideal with reality); to cause to submit or to accept.

The only way for us to restore friendships between one another and settle differences with God is to accept the principle of forgiveness. As the church, we are charged to go to the world and extend the same level of forgiveness to it as God extended to us for the purpose of making things congruous between heaven and earth again.

THE EFFECTS OF UNFORGIVENESS ON THE SOUL

There's a progression of symptoms that reside in the soul when we choose to reject forgiveness. The first is self-judgment. Self-judgment has many aliases and alliances: guilt, shame, subconscious self-punishment, condemnation, to name a few. Romans 8:1-2 infers that the latter of these is directly linked to the law of sin and death. Since its inception, the law of sin and death has tempted us to futilely strive as we live for a place of perfection; fearing the moment that we don't measure up to this expectation which then warrants our unworthiness for love and approval. But beloved, we came into the world unworthy! We came into the world imperfect to help resolve the source of its imperfection: sin. Though God's plan appeared to have been thwarted, Christ eventually came to satisfy the law of sin and death through exchanging the need for human strength with the power of His resurrected life! A power that was then extended to the world through the Holy Spirit.

> **"And if Christ be in you, the body is dead because of sin; but the Spirit is life because of righteousness. But if the Spirit of him that raised up Jesus from the dead dwell in you, he that raised up Christ from the dead shall also quicken your mortal bodies by his Spirit that dwells in you."**
>
> **– Romans 8:10-11**

We no longer need to subject ourselves to the "religious duty" of self-flagellation due to our innate drive to live up to being accepted as His Beloved because Jesus already did that for us! He became the perfect substitute in Spirit for the imperfect substance of our flesh. Once we understand this, we can be awakened to our fullness in Jesus. Once awakened to our fullness in Jesus, we can then release the Holy Spirit to live in our soul through perpetual forgiveness. Once we've released the Holy Spirit to live in our souls, we are equipped to extend Him to others. On the other hand, when we reject forgiveness, we're releasing darkness to reside in our soul by default.

Several of us were praying for some women at a conference once. One woman was escorted to our team while she was weeping due to the emotional pain and torment that she had been experiencing which she was ready to release. As we began talking to her, she continually repeated the following phrase to us:

"I need deliverance."

After we assured her that she had been delivered by the Blood of Jesus and began praying for her, the Holy Spirit revealed that there were two men she needed to forgive. I mentioned this to her and she began to share the pain and rejection that she experienced from both her current and ex-husband. We led her through a forgiveness prayer and in less than 30 minutes, she went from repeating the need to be delivered to "I'm free!" This woman's countenance completely changed as she expressed the peace and joy that she was experiencing. Nothing in her circumstances had changed, but she had released herself and the two men from captivity which changed her whole perspective and emotional state of mind.

"Now the Lord is that Spirit: and where the Spirit of the Lord is, there is liberty."
– 2 Corinthians 3:17

Again, self-judgment is a result of not receiving forgiveness from God and not feeling worthy of His forgiveness. If we don't believe that we're worthy of receiving His forgiveness, we'll sabotage (consciously or subconsciously) our lives and relationships in various ways as we beat ourselves up – thus the aforementioned self-flagellation. Such self-judgment is destructive for our lives in body, soul and spirit. If I may briefly exercise my prerogative as an author, I'd like to expound about the importance of the Blood of Christ mentioned at the beginning of this story – specifically as it relates to believers. By His Blood, we have been made worthy of forgiveness but by not rejecting the totality of this forgiveness, we're rejecting the totality of the Blood of Christ. Doing so essentially expresses either an unbelief in or irrelevance in His resurrection after the crucifixion. Either way, this makes a mockery of the work Jesus performed on the Cross.

Moving on, yet another adverse effect of unforgiveness is confusion between God's law of love and man's law of religious works. If I can speak to self-flagellation again – this was actually an accepted act of penance practiced not only by a sect of the Roman Catholic Church but by Martin Luther himself – the father of the Protestant Reformation! The deceptive confusion of God's law and man's law can lead us back to seeking natural methods (carnal weapons) and physical acts to remedy our sins. Moreover, this extends the mockery of the final work of Jesus Christ. How, you ask? Whipping (physical or figuratively) yourself implies that the stripes of Christ were not enough. After all, what are we saying seems easier when asked to choose between the two: examining the heart and inviting the Spirit of God to heal the soul or beating ourselves up? Which seems easier to you? Psychology calls such striving behavioral modification; but attempting to modify behavior from the outside is short-lived and does nothing for the heart. Instead, it leads to futility and hopelessness until we understand that we can't acquire what Jesus already accomplished for us.

I once had a client who struggled with anxiety. She and her mother had come to me to get both a stress assessment and coping skills to help her deal with the pressure of being successful at school. It just so happened that she had been a runner for a season in her life but had to stop due to an overuse of her ankle. Overuse comes from rigorous performance which can stress the ankles of a runner. My client's drive to be seen and known (or rather, her "overdrive") put undue pressure on not just her ankle as she became motivated by the fear of not measuring up to her own high expectations. The Holy Spirit used that to *relay* to her the real source of her stress: the overuse of her mind attempting to compensate for what the pressures of college life had placed on her. Once I explained to her that her value had nothing to do with her performance and that she was worthy without doing anything, I pulled out "old faithful" on her:

"Who are you?"

Upon her telling me she was a hard worker and me telling her to separate what she does from who she is, she described herself using such words as "kind, determined and deep." These types of words are applicable whether you're working hard or hardly working which skirts the need for her to condemn herself in times when no amount of work seems hard enough.

This particular client described herself from where forgiveness begins: the heart. This is also the place where long-lasting change takes place. For example, you can attempt to heal anger through an education group that dissects what makes a person angry then teaches said person how to change their thinking to avoid such anger. That may bring some temporary relief... or you can walk the person through forgiveness (of self and others) and watch their heart heal from the inside out as their behaviors resolve themselves. Within the educational approach, unforgiveness keeps the mind in captivity which is why the behavior changes won't last long. Einstein said it best:

"You can't solve the problem on the same level it was created."

Returning to the juxtaposition of God's law of love versus man's law and the negative effects of the latter on the soul; self-righteousness is one of the most repugnant ways to smudge the state of the soulish man. When we seek to be justified not by faith in Jesus but by the law of man, we have set ourselves up for failure. Though father of the Protestant Reformation may have gotten it wrong with the whole self-flagellation routine, he literally nailed it when he bet his reputation by splitting from the Catholic Church based on Ephesians 2:8-9 which stated:

"For by grace are ye saved through faith; and that not of yourselves: it is the gift of God: Not of works, lest any man should boast."

Our justification is a gift that no works of ours can add to or subtract from; yet and still, people will try to live according to what the law has stated they can earn in their own strength. This is the source of self-righteousness: pretending as if we've been perfected and are capable of living without sin. The only power found in this is one that has managed to destroy the image of the church; making it appear as if Christians and God are judgmental and condemning. All this accomplishes is a merit-based system for getting (and allowing others to get) into a relationship with God – as if our humanity wasn't already flawed and in need of what Christ came to do for us which had everything to do with proving God's unconditional love… and that my soul knows right well.

JUDGING: THE BIGGEST BLINDER TO FORGIVENESS

Judging others bears the trappings of self-righteousness, pride and division. We don't know the justification process that God has for someone else unless we're able to acknowledge a process of forgiveness we've gone through. Recalling that God looks at those in Christ as a finished product in eternity, it should allow us to look at each other (if only for a glimpse of someone else's eternity) the same was, as well.

In John 8:1, after the woman was caught in adultery, those

who caught her were reminding Jesus of the Law of Moses (man) and demanded a response. However, the response they got reflected the law of love. As they were demanding justice for her indiscretion, Jesus chose to rise above it. As He bent down in a gesture that they thought would be the precursor to stoning her, Jesus simply wrote in the dust with His finger (the same finger Moses used to introduce the law). I believe what He wrote was an allusion to the prophecy of Jeremiah 17:13 which points to those who have forsaken God (thus committing *spiritual* adultery) being written in the dust. Spiritual adultery, defined as putting anything above or before God, has always been a serious offense to God.

Jesus, Who came to show people the love of God, eloquently showed how judging another person for their behavior and putting that above love is an offense to which they had become blind. Of course, He accented the offense by putting the ball back in their court by inviting the man who had no sinful desire in his heart to cast the first stone. Did you see what He did, though? He went to the law of the heart. He emphasized the fact that sin is a condition of man's heart being incongruent with God's heart. And try as we might, none of our hearts (born into sin) are able to align to His righteousness of our own accord. Thus, not one of us claiming and feigning to be innocent can judge another, unless we open the door to being judged under false pretense.

FORGIVENESS PRAYER

"Heavenly Father, In The Name of Jesus Christ, I confess, repent, and renounce unforgiveness and thank You that You're a forgiving Father. From this day forward, I purpose and choose from my heart and with my will and emotions to forgive **[name of offender]** for what s/he did. Also, from this day forward, I choose to release him/her from all judgment and condemnation from me and I cancel every debt s/he owes to me. In the name of Jesus Christ, I also cancel all of satan's authority in this memory because it's forgiven. In the name of Jesus Christ, I command all of the anger, pain, etc. to go, in the name of Jesus Christ and never return! Holy Spirit, heal my heart. Occupy every vacancy vacated by darkness and fill me up with Your love, light and truth.

Bless **[name of FORMER offender being forgiven]**"

(Portions taken from Art Mathias, Biblical Foundations Of Freedom)

CONCLUSION

Healing for individuals and for the church as a body will not happen without each of us individually and corporately making the decision to be intentionally connected. This book is a call for the "body" to come together and begin incorporating these principles. The process begins with an open dialogue about each of these principles and determining where to continue afterwards.

So as I thank you for taking the time to read my musings, I challenge you to start the conversation in your community about reconciliation from God's perspective with an emphasis on the expectation of healing. Please don't simply mark this book as another notch on the belt you've read without exploring and acting on how you plan to contribute to the dismantling of separation among your fellow neighbors, countrymen and children of God throughout the world. It starts with each of us being willing to take an honest look at the condition of our own health and heart. If you're not satisfied with the current condition of any standing relationships, partner with someone to address the issue. If you are satisfied, help the body deepen the roots of its reconciliation by sharing your testimony so that more people can reap the benefit of your fruit for the glory of God.

REFERENCES

BIBLIOGRAPHY:

1) Alexander, Eben. *Proof of Heaven: A Neurosurgeon's Journey into the Afterlife*. New York. Simon & Shuster Paperbacks, 2012. Print.The Holy Bible: New International Version. Grand Rapids, MI: Zondervan, 1996.

2) Benner, David G. *The Gift of Being Yourself: The Sacred Call to Self-Discovery*. Downers Grove. InterVarsity Press, 2004. Print.

3) The Holy Bible: New Revised Standard Version. Nashville, TN: Thomas Nelson Publishers, 1989.

4) Jennings, Timothy R. *The God Shaped Brain: How Changing Your View of God, Transforms Your Life*. Downers Grove: InterVarsity Press, 2013. Print.

5) *Journal of Personal Relationships.* 2011. Print.

6) *Journal of Psychological Science.* 2001. Print.

7) Lehman, Karl D. *The Immanuel Approach: For Emotional Healing and for Life.* Immanuel Publishing, 2016. Print.

8) Newberg, Andrew and Mark R. Waldman. *How God Changes Your Brain.* New York: Ballantine Books, 2010. Print.

9) Swartz, Karen. "The Healing Power of Forgiveness." *Johns Hopkins Health.* Baltimore: JHM Publications. www.hopkinsmedicine.org.

10) Web. 2014. ten Boom, Corrie, *The Hiding Place.* Grand Rapids: Chosen Books, 2006. Print.

11) Hew Len, Ihaleakala and Joe Vitale. *Zero Limits: The Secret Hawaiian System for Wealth, Health, Peace, and More.* Hoboken: John Wiley & Sons, 2010. Print.

12) Warner, Marcus and Jim Wilder. *Rare Leadership: 4 Uncommon Habits For Increasing Trust, Joy, and Engagement in the People You Lead.* Chicago. Moody Publishers, 2016. Print.

ONLINE:

1) The Holy Bible. Amplified Version. Biblica, 2011. www.blueletterbible.com/versions/Amplified-Version-AMP-Bible

2) The Holy Bible. King James Version. Biblica, 2011. www.blueletterbible/versions/King-James-Version-KJV-Bible

3) The Holy Bible. The Message. Biblica, 2011. www.blueletterbible/versions/Message-Version-MES-Bible

4) The Holy Bible. New International Version. Biblica, 2011. www.blueletterbible/versions/New-International-Version-NIV-Bible

5) Insel, Thomas R., Young, Larry J. "The Neurobiology of Attachment." *Nature Reviews* Feb. 2001. *Nature.com* Web. VOL 2.

6) Merriam Webster's Dictionary. 2018. www.merriam-webster.com